The Kogan Page Market Research Series breaks new ground in market research publishing. While most books tend to be all embracing tomes covering every aspect of market research, each title in this new series is devoted to a specific technique or key area.

The prime aim of the titles in the series is to demystify the technicalities of market research by providing concise, digestible introductions, presented in a clear and comprehensive style.

Well-illustrated throughout, these practical guides will serve as vital introductions for those new to market research, useful revision tools for students and essential refreshers for all market research professionals.

Titles in the series are:

> *Questionnaire Design*
> *Interviewing*
> *Sampling and Statistics*
> *Desk Research*

Future titles will cover:

> Reporting and presenting data
> Analysis and modelling

DESK RESEARCH

Peter Jackson

KOGAN
PAGE

First published in 1994

Kogan Page Limited
120 Pentonville Road
London N1 9JN

British Library Cataloguing in Publication Data
A CIP record for this book is available from the British Library.
ISBN 0 7494 1217 8

Typeset by BookEns Limited, Baldock, Herts.
Printed in England by Clays Ltd, St Ives plc

CONTENTS

■

ABOUT THE AUTHOR

■

Peter Jackson has 25 years' practical experience of market research, the majority of this time as a director of Business and Market Research plc. He is the joint author of *How to do Marketing Research*, *Do Your Own Market Research* and *Marketing Research in Practice*, all published by Kogan Page. He also writes on wider management issues.

PREFACE

■

I have worked in market research since the 1960s and over the years spent many, many hours in libraries carrying out desk research. Looking back, however, I was never shown how to set about the task. I just picked up knowledge, in a fragmented way, as I went along. My systematic approach to desk research evolved slowly and, I now recognise, inefficiently. Yet the principles of carrying out desk research are simple. I hope that this book will provide the sort of introduction to desk research as a practical activity, which, in retrospect, I wish I had been given.

This book is part of *The Market Research Series*. No prior knowledge of either desk research or the wider area of market research is assumed. It can be read alone, although anyone with an interest in desk research is likely to find other useful titles in the series.

Today, desk research increasingly involves accessing on-line databases and this aspect of desk research is covered, and particulary in Chapter 10. I would like to thank my colleague, Mark Tipping, for reading through and giving advice on that chapter. Any faults are mine and not his. Thanks also to Liz Jackson for helping to tidy up the manuscript.

In preparing the book, I made considerable use of Manchester Central Library which provides an excellent and well stocked commercial section and whose staff are really helpful. I hope that the value of this and similar libraries will continue to be recognised and supported by fund providers. Libraries, open to all, are a vital and cost-effective part of the knowledge industry.

Peter Jackson
October 1993

1

INTRODUCTION

■

Desk research is a rather neglected part of market research. There are many source books providing references for marketing data and quite a few are mentioned in this book, but little is written on desk research as an activity and subject.

Part of the problem may be that desk research lacks glamour. Few reputations have been built on desk research alone — how many famous desk researchers have you heard of? One factor may be that market research agencies — and the trendsetters mainly work in agencies — are, generally, little involved in desk research. There are commercial reasons why this is so (see Chapter 2).

Desk research is a common activity of 'in house', as opposed to agency, researchers. Indeed, desk research is often the only form of research carried out, rather than commissioned, 'in house'. With limited staff, field research on any scale is just not practical in house, but many information needs can be met through desk research. This type of data collection is well within the practical scope of even a lone researcher and requires few additional, if any, resources. Arguably, if more or more and better desk research was undertaken, less field research would be needed and market research budgets would be more effectively and efficiently spent. There would be less wastage of resources (including responses to surveys) from commissioning expensive research where much of the required data is already available and accessible.

There is also little formal training given in desk research. The subject is seldom offered as a training course and may be barely mentioned in general introduction seminars. More often, the 'new boy' or 'new girl' is given a desk research project as a first task (it will keep them out of mischief for a week or so) but are then left to their own devices and have to learn the basics of desk research as they go along. Part of the problem is that there is an erroneous assumption that anyone with even half an education will know how to build up an analysis of a market from library sources.

On-line database searching is another matter. The dangers and potential costs of letting a novice play with a database are usually recognised and some training will be given or arranged. However, the focus tends to be the mechanical side of using databases — the command structure and so on — rather than the wider scope of this type of source and its links into the subject of desk research. Without an adequate understanding of the major sources available, whether on-line or in conventional form, database users can become mere button-pushers and fail to realise the enormous information potential which, with the right knowledge, can be tapped.

This book has been written to provide both a practical guide to new researchers (or the more experienced who have not as yet, been involved in desk research) and to show how desk research, as an activity, fits into market research as a whole. The next chapter briefly discusses the role of market research and how it is carried out. Desk research is then distinguished from other methods of collecting data. Chapter 2 also stresses the importance of setting objectives for research.

Chapter 3 introduces the scope of information that is available from desk research and, equally, what cannot be found in this way. An overview of the sources of information are provided in Chapter 4 with fuller detail covered, by broad subject areas, in the following four chapters — the marketing environment (Chapter 5), market analysis — including sizing markets (Chapter 6), information on companies (Chapter 7) and products (Chapter 8).

Up to this point in the book, UK market data is the principal concern. However, markets are increasingly international and desk research is particularly cost-effective for overseas research. Chapter 9 covers this important part of desk research.

Throughout the book, on-line database sources are mentioned as appropriate. Accessing marketing information in this way is now a routine part of the desk research process. Chapter 10 describes the principles of on-line databases and provides practical guidance on getting started in this type of desk research.

Finally a chapter is given to the important topic of reporting — unless data is adequately communicated it is worthless. Chapter 11 covers both special problems in reporting desk research and some of the general principles of preparing effective written reports or making face-to-face presentations.

This is not a source book — it is not a comprehensive listing of information sources relevant to market research. There are many excellent guides and directories of this type and several are recommended at appropriate points. However, some sources are given throughout the book. In many cases these references illustrate a point made in the text and there is no intention to provide full listings in any area. The omission of a source, therefore, has no particular significance. References are printed in italics — eg *Business Monitor*[1] in the text and are listed by number, together with contact details, at the end of the book — in Chapter 12.

2

THE ROLE OF
DESK RESEARCH

■

This chapter defines desk research and shows how it fits into the wider market research process.

The need for market research is considered first and then the process is described. A key part of the process is collecting primary and secondary data. Desk research is concerned with accessing published, secondary data and this is discussed. The skills and resources required for desk research are also covered in this chapter.

RESEARCH FOR MARKETING DECISIONS

Managers make decisions; a good manager is one who makes good decisions. The basis of good decisions is having appropriate information available and using it effectively. This applies throughout all functions of a business or other organisation including finance, production and personnel. Our interest, however, is in the marketing function.

A common type of marketing decision is deciding what should be done with a product producing a below average or unsatisfactory profit. In principle there are three strategies which can be considered alone or in combination and these are shown in Table 2.1. For each strategy, information is required before an informed decision can be made. The table also shows some (but not an exhaustive list of) relevant marketing information for each of the three strategies.

TABLE 2.1 MARKETING STRATEGIES AND INFORMATION TO INCREASE THE PROFITABILITY OF A PRODUCT

Strategy	Marketing Information
Sell more	Size of total market for the product Our share of the product Availability of our product (retail penetration) Consumer awareness of our product Consumer acceptance and attitudes to our product
Charge more	Competitive pricing levels Consumer perception of the relative value of our product Likely effect of price increase on sales volumes
Cut costs	Whether any product reformulation has a negative effect on consumer perceptions Effect on distribution

Market research is concerned with providing decision makers with the type of information illustrated in Table 2.1. To be effective such information has to be reliable and accurate (or at least to within known levels of accuracy) and over the last half century market research has become a formal business discipline with its own theories, techniques and standards. Market research is also a business with some 300 commercial companies in the UK offering this type of service. It is also carried out 'in house' by marketing organisations, often as a part time activity by staff with wider responsibilities. Market research may be carried out on a 'do it yourself' basis by the manager making the decision, although there is a good case for independence wherever possible — there is the ever present danger of looking for information to back the decision that the manager would 'like' to make.

THE MARKET RESEARCH PROCESS

Any collection of facts relevant to a marketing decision can be considered to be market research. However, we are concerned

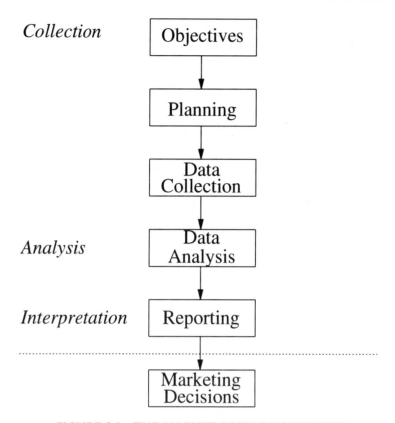

FIGURE 2.1   THE MARKET RESEARCH PROCESS

with something rather more than an occasional and haphazard use of snippets. A formal definition of the market research process can be as follows.

Market Research — the systematic collection, analysis and interpretation of information relevant to marketing decisions.

Market research can be carried out as a once-off project (ad-hoc research) to meet a specific requirement — eg whether or not to enter a new market — or can involve continuous or regular tracking — eg to monitor the market share held by a product. In either case the process involved is in principle the same, and is illustrated in Figure 2.1.

A market research project must always have a defined *objective*; however fascinating an activity it is not carried out for its own sake. Going back to the example in Table 2.1, an objective may be:

> To provide information relevant to deciding how we can increase the profitability of the product.

With some such suitable statement of objectives the company or staff carrying out the research know what they are meant to achieve and the 'clients' — the managers responsible for making decisions — know what to expect at the end of the exercise. Obviously both parties need to agree the objective.

As in any activity, success in a market research process depends on *planning*. This includes defining the information required to meet the objective — Table 2.1 lists some relevant information to meet the above objective — deciding on appropriate methods to collect the information and how this data will be analysed and reported to the client. Since market research takes place in a commercial environment, planning will also involve deciding a budget for the work — what is appropriate relative to the commercial importance of the decision or more commonly what can be afforded — and a timetable. Where the research is carried out by a commercial research company the objectives and at least the broad planning of the work will be set out in a proposal document at the quotation stage and even an in house project should involve a written statement of objectives and research plan, however brief a document.

The *data collection* part of the process is discussed in more detail below. This is often the visible part of market research — the interviewer in the shopping precinct pestering time-pressed shoppers to help with 'just a few questions'. However, the immediate outcome of this is raw data which, as it stands, is of no use whatsoever. The data must be processed in the *analysis* stage. Analysis involves tasks such as aggregating data (eg individual responses provided in each interview), statistical manipulation and fitting disparate facts together to provide the basis of a coherent whole. Often the analysis of primary data (see below) involves standardised computer processing using specialised software with statistical tables as the outcome. Other types of data may involve more individual analysis work (eg merging statistics from two different sources) and the line between analysis and reporting is often vague. *Reporting* involves both assembling the processed data into a 'user friendly' form and interpretation — these are the facts, now what relevance do they have to the marketing decision? The effective researcher makes a report in a form which the decision maker can easily assimilate and relate to the decisions that have to be made. The format of the report can be varied according to the situation and may be largely verbal backed by charts rather than a full blown narrative document. The report may include recommendations — what the researcher believes should be done — but the final responsibility for the decision rests with the 'client' manager.

DATA COLLECTION

Data collection includes the process of obtaining both primary and secondary data as set out in Figure 2.2.

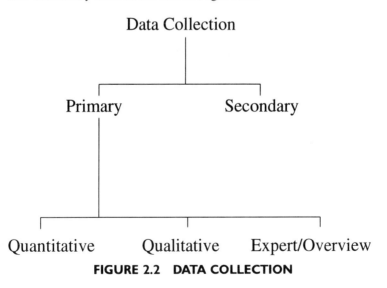

FIGURE 2.2   DATA COLLECTION

Primary data is collected specially, by the researcher, to meet the particular information needs of the project — eg I need to establish the competitive pricing of a series of books so I visit a number of bookshops and record which publications are on the shelves (perhaps with details of binding, format and length) and the selling prices. In this case the primary data is collected by observation but in market research the most common technique is the questioning of relevant respondents (interviewing). The figure breaks down primary research into three sub-categories and very briefly these are as follows.

■ **Quantitative**. Collecting data from a controlled and representative sample using a standardised questionnaire or record sheet. Specific techniques include face-to-face or phone interviewing, postal surveys or observation (eg retail checks).

■ **Qualitative**. Interviews in depth, usually with a small sample of respondents. The subject matter is usually concerned with attitudes, perceptions or motivation and may be one to one or involve a guided group discussion (focus groups).

■ **Expert/Overview**. In the above cases the responses from individuals are aggregated to provide an overall picture. Expert or overview interviews involve a meeting with an individual who has an overview of a whole subject (he or she may well have carried out relevant research). This type of data collection is more related to journalism than formal market research but it can certainly have an important role in some types of projects.

Whatever its form, primary research involves collecting information to meet a specific purpose and in principle the data does not exist until we go out and collect it by interview or whatever method. *Secondary data* already exists and has been collected in the past for some purpose quite unconnected to our project — eg a previous survey of the book trade includes data on the size of the retail market for all business books split by discipline, although the breakdown may go no further than 'marketing' rather than 'market research' publications. While, therefore, primary data matches our requirements by design, any match in the case of

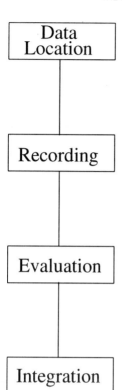

FIGURE 2.3   THE DESK RESEARCH PROCESS

secondary data is more a matter of chance and luck; this is one of its problems. It is worth remembering that in most cases secondary data was originally obtained using the methods appropriate for primary data, usually by some sort of interview.

ACCESSING SECONDARY DATA THROUGH DESK RESEARCH

Desk research (and at last we come to the subject of this book) is the process of accessing *published* secondary data. The term 'published' is used in the widest sense to include not only books and journals but also many databases, reports sold at relatively high prices and the results of various continuous surveys available to subscribers. Data such as these are collected either with the intention of publishing or are published as a spin-off from some original purpose. The proceeds of publishing contribute to or cover the cost of collecting the data. The process of desk research — accessing published secondary data — is represented in Figure 2.3.

The sources of secondary data through desk research are discussed in detail in subsequent chapters but include newspapers and journals, directories, reports, government statistics, statistics published by other bodies such as trade associations and company accounts (and the various services based on company accounts). The first step in the desk research process is to locate the sources relevant to a particular project. This may involve any of the following:

- **In-house files.** Often relevant data is in the filing cabinet waiting to be used. They may have been collected for a specific purpose or just because someone thought it interesting.
- **Libraries.** Visits to libraries were until recently the core activity of desk research. The larger and more specialised libraries contain an enormous range of published secondary data. Part of the skill of desk research is knowing how to use libraries to locate relevant sources. Using the various indexes of published data, consulting sources of sources, asking for help from staff and just browsing the shelves are all methods of locating sources and are discussed in more detail in Chapter 4 and subsequently.
- **Database searching.** The electronic equivalent to visiting libraries is to access databases from your own desk. This will not only identify sources but also the substantive information. It should be noted that the sources are largely the same whether accessed in traditional 'paper' form or on-screen. Electronic databases are discussed briefly in Chapter 4 and in more detail in Chapter 10. Since, however, conventional and database sources are often the same, other chapters are relevant to databases as well.
- **Buying-in data.** The more expensive published sources are usually not available in libraries and must be bought-in.

These include the many market research reports published speculatively at prices from a few hundred to several thousand pounds. Such data can be located through specialised directories and databases.

■ **Collecting free information.** Much useful information can be collected from the publishing organisations for the cost of a phone call or letter. Examples include the reports of large public companies and product literature.

Once sources are located, the relevant data must be recorded either by note taking or copying. In the case of database access, the equivalent is transferring to a computer file or printing out as hard copy.

Just because information is printed or on a database it is not necessarily reliable. Before the results of desk research are used they should be evaluated. This is discussed in Chapter 3. Finally the disparate strands of data and possibly the results of primary research carried out for a project need to be integrated and presented as a clear report to decision makers. Chapter 11 deals with reporting.

THE INTERRELATION OF PRIMARY AND SECONDARY DATA

In many market research projects both primary and secondary data sources will be needed to meet the objectives of the research. In research to evaluate the marketing potential of an acquisition, the size, structure and possibly market share held of the relevant market may be obtainable through desk research but other information — eg the reputation and image of the company in its market — will require primary research to be undertaken. In general it is the best approach to carry out desk research before planning any primary research. Primary research is nearly always more expensive than carrying out desk research and, therefore, there is a strong argument for limiting its scope to data that cannot be obtained more cheaply from published sources. However, timetable constraints may make it impractical to delay starting primary research until desk research has been completed although this is probably exceptional because while efficient desk research should take only a few days, a programme of interviews often takes weeks to plan, carry out and process the resulting data.

Another problem with following the desk research first rule lies with the commercial relationship between research companies and their clients. Typically clients ask research companies to propose and quote for a project before any preliminary research has been done in house. The lack of resources within the client company may well be why a commercial research company is being approached. Unless the project is very large, the research company cannot afford to spend unpaid time carrying out preliminary desk research before preparing the proposal document. Consequently assumptions have to be made about what is likely to be available from desk research and what will require interviewing or other primary research. An experienced researcher can in fact often make a realistic judgement but the tendency is to play safe and assume that relevant secondary data is not available. Moreover, the charges and profits that can be made for primary research are generally higher than for desk research. This is both because primary research *is* more expensive to carry out but also because clients tend to discount the value of desk research and are less willing to pay realistically for this part of a research company's service.

There is also the problem for the research company that the outcome of desk research is often uncertain until it is carried out and there is a reluctance to offer and charge for a service that may produce little that it useful to the client. In contrast the outcome of primary research is generally predictable — I know that if I design an appropriate questionnaire, the data covered can be collected through the interviewing process. The consequence of all this is that much time is spent and paid for 'reinventing the wheel'. Often clients would be better asking for desk research to be carried out as a separate, initial part of the project before commitment to primary research. Where research is carried out in house, these problems do not usually arise.

Not only is it usually cheaper to carry out desk research before primary research, it may be essential. In business to business research for example, a representative programme of interviews can only be set up after data is obtained on the structure of the market being surveyed. In contrast to consumer research, each consumption unit — each establishment — is very definitely not of equal importance. More likely a handful of the largest companies account for a very large percentage of the particular market with perhaps a hundred smaller firms sharing out the rest (the 80:20 Pareto rule). This must be understood and the large companies identified before any fieldwork is attempted. Desk research will usually provide the necessary picture of the market structure. Similarly, in consumer research, the demographic profile of the population being surveyed may be required to plan fieldwork and set quotas (for a quota sample). The population may be all of a country, a region or buyers of certain products. In each case demographic data can be obtained from desk research.

SKILLS AND RESOURCES FOR DESK RESEARCH

The resources required for primary research can be extensive. For an interviewing programme of any size, a team of interviewers will have to be recruited, briefed and possibly trained. Data processing facilities are likely to be required on completion of the interviews. Even qualitative research — groups or depth interviews — although carried out by one person, are likely to require several interviewers to work on recruitment. For these reasons primary research is seldom within the practical capabilities of a small in house department and involvement in this area will generally be limited to commissioning outside research companies. By contrast little is required for desk research. One person can usually cover the ground very adequately and in the case of 'conventional' desk research the only resource needed is access to an adequate library; at least one is likely to be within 50 miles of any UK office base. Database searching does require a PC (personal computer) with the facility to link into, by phone, the available databases but by now anyone contemplating desk research is likely to have a PC available that can be cheaply adapted with a modem link (see Chapters 4 and 10 for further discussion of this topic).

The really essential resource for successful desk research is human; the researcher's skill in the work. Hopefully this book will provide some of these skills, including methods of locating secondary data, using databases and planning the work. No special aptitude is required to acquire these skills although a certain perseverance is useful (as is knowing when to abandon a search because of diminishing returns from further time and effort). However, some of the skills can only come from experience of the sources and the process of their location.

Compared with primary research, desk research generally is cheap. However, some of the costs are often hidden since they arise from staff time spent on the process. A few days of skilled research staff time can be significant even though it may not be a formally costed overhead. The costs of using databases, in contrast, are explicit since the 'host' bills you on a time basis. When first used, such charges can be high both because of a lack of experience in carrying out efficient searches and because novelty leads to unwise applications. Bought-in reports and other data of this type also have a quite significant cost but in this case the charges are known in advance and can be weighed against the likely benefits from the data.

3

INFORMATION AVAILABLE FROM DESK RESEARCH

∎

Desk research can provide a very wide range of marketing information. This chapter discusses the broad topics which are commonly covered in market research projects and indicates which are likely to be accessible through desk research and which are not. Some sources are mentioned in passing but details of where and how to find data are covered in the next and later chapters.

CONSUMER AND INDUSTRIAL MARKET RESEARCH

The most general classification of marketing information is between consumer and industrial markets. Consumer markets are for goods and services which you and I buy personally — eg food and other fmcgs (fast moving consumer goods), home appliances, clothes, cars, holidays and personal financial services. In contrast the buying unit in industrial markets is an organisation — a company, a public body etc. The products and services may be technical and 'industrial' in a strict sense — eg raw materials such as steel or oil, machinery or plant maintenance services, or used in offices — eg paper, office equipment, courier services and telecommunications. The term business to business is often used to describe this sort of market (and may be used interchangeably with 'industrial'). Some products and services are used in both types of markets although are often marketed in different forms (eg paper products, property insurance). A few specialised markets do not fit happily in either the consumer or industrial classification; medical and pharmaceutical are the best example.

Both consumer and industrial markets can be covered in desk research and extensive sources are available for both areas. In some cases the sources overlap — eg government statistics — but often a source and a provider of data deals with only one of the two major types of market. As mentioned in the introduction, this book is aimed at both consumer and industrial market researchers and covers in later chapters relevant sources and approaches for both types of market.

AD HOC AND CONTINUOUS RESEARCH

Desk research has a place in both ad hoc and continuous market research. Ad hoc research is carried out from scratch. After the objective of the research has been defined and a plan drawn up, including a list of the information needed to meet the objective, the desk research task is first to locate relevant sources of data. Later knowledge gaps may be filled through primary research. In contrast, once initial work has been carried out, any relevant sources for continuous research will be known and the task is only one of regular collection. Data on market size, brand shares, activities of suppliers, retail distribution and much else can, in particular markets, be collected and updated at regular intervals from published sources. Quite possibly, a continuous research project is built around the data available and although it does not provide all the information required to track a market, it is of sufficient value to set up a system to collect regularly the up-to-date published information. This may involve a standing sub-scription for the relevant sources (eg *Business Monitors*[1]).

DOMESTIC AND OVERSEAS MARKETS

Desk research can be used to collect data on overseas as well as domestic markets. Data on overseas markets may be at an individual country, world region or grouping (eg EEC) or whole world level. The basic sources of information are generally corespondingly similar. All the developed countries at least, for example, have government statistics comparable to those produced by the British government. Similarly international bodies such as the EEC Commission, the UN and the OECD publish vast quantities of statistical and other data of interest in many research projects. Other broad groups of sources eg the press, directories, company accounts are all available in some form for international market research. Arguably, desk research is a particularly appropriate method for international research. Often budget limitations are such that primary research cannot be afforded for overseas markets and in practice information has to be limited to published sources.

The major sources and approaches for desk research are covered in Chapters 4 to 8 and in each the focus is the UK market. Comments on overseas desk research and sources are then discussed in Chapter 9. For the purposes of this book, EEC countries apart from the UK are regarded, despite the single market, as 'foreign'.

TYPES OF MARKETING INFORMATION AVAILABLE THROUGH DESK RESEARCH

We shall now indicate what types of information can realistically be sought through desk research and what can not. The following is a listing of the broad types of information commonly required in market research although in no one study would all or even most of it be relevant.

- The marketing environment.
- A market and its structure.
- Suppliers and brands.
- Distribution and retailing.
- Products and new product development.
- Pricing.
- Marketing methods and advertising.

We shall look in more detail at each of these categories of information and in general terms consider the likelihood of obtaining useful data through desk research.

THE MARKETING ENVIRONMENT

The markets for particular products or services do not exist in a vacuum and are influenced and often determined by wider economic or social factors eg:

■　The macro economy:
　　—GDP
　　—Output
　　—Exports, imports and balance of trade
　　—Price trends.
■　Economic analysis of major sectors — manufacturing, services etc.
■　Demographic trends.
■　Lifestyle analysis.
■　Ownership of major products.
■　Transport.
■　Housing.

Obviously the general level of prosperity effects the demand for a very wide range of both consumer and industrial goods. Similarly a specific market for a product may be shaped by trends within the economic sector it is part of or supplies — eg the brick market will obviously be linked to the level and nature of the construction industry. Demographic trends too shape markets — eg trends towards women working outside the home may create market opportunities in retailing, convenience foods and financial services. Also some products are complementary to others and an understanding of the linked market may be required for a meaningful analysis — eg trends in original specification of cars and the market for accessories.

Desk research is often the only practical method of providing data on the wider marketing environment. Also the level of documentation in both the UK and overseas in these areas is high and for most purposes there is more than enough accessible data. Often the problem is one of selection; an analysis of a market perhaps should mention the links to the wider economy but a detailed analysis of the UK economy over the last 20 years is not called for. The major sources for the marketing environment include government statistics and commentaries on this sort of data. These and others are discussed in Chapter 5.

A MARKET AND ITS STRUCTURE

A company considering entry into a new market or assessing its position within its established business is likely to require market research covering such topics as:-

■ Market size, sectors and niches.
■ Profile of consumers.
■ Their needs and requirements.
■ Major players in the market and their shares — manufacturers, importers.
■ Branding.
■ Consumer awareness and attitudes to brands.
■ Trends in size of market and its structure, seasonality.

The availability of published data on market size varies widely. However, much of the required data for major consumer products and services is available, particularly in medium price published reports as well as by subscription to continuous research. Some of this material may be accessible free of charge in libraries. Also the general and trade press often carry reports containing some of the relevant data — again usually accessible free of charge. Documentation of industrial markets is also good and usually desk research can be used to at least estimate market size. Also there may well be relevant published reports dealing with a particular industrial market.

In both consumer and industrial markets, a thorough understanding requires data on the consumers; who they are, what their needs and requirements are and their awareness and attitudes to brands. Consumer profiles may be available from published reports but attitudinal data — motivations, needs and perceptions are likely to be much sparser and these are the areas where primary research may be needed to obtain a full understanding. Data on consumer attitudes is important, especially where the intention is to develop new products to better meet consumers' needs.

Sources on a market and its structure are covered in detail in Chapter 6.

SUPPLIERS AND BRANDS

Data on suppliers can be considered an extension of the market information discussed above and includes:

■ Profiles of major suppliers and their brands.
■ Their marketing methods and advertising.
■ Factors making for success (and failure).
■ Consumer attitudes to suppliers — companies' images, customer satisfaction.

An understanding of the potential competition is as important as market size etc when deciding on a market entry or other strategy. However, understanding consumer and customer attitudes to suppliers — including your own company — can also be the key objective of a research study; so-called image research and customer satisfaction research. The availability of published data is broadly similar to the position for market data. In both consumer and industrial markets, published reports may well profile suppliers and perhaps provide some data on marketing methods. This can be supplemented by financial analysis from company accounts and the sources which analyse and provide this data. The suppliers' own publicity material may also provide some information on marketing methods although much is often invisible. Some aspects of advertising are well documented but *how* campaigns work and their relative effectiveness are usually only accessible through primary research. Similarly little is usually available through desk research on attitudes to specific suppliers and obviously not on your own company. Desk research is unlikely to have much role in image or customer satisfaction research.

The sources for supplier information are covered in Chapter 7.

DISTRIBUTION AND RETAILING

Virtually all consumer markets have an established retail structure including:

■ The network structure.
■ Stocking and ordering practices.
■ Distribution levels achieved.
■ Attitudes to suppliers.
■ Retail and distributor marketing.

These are well documented in published reports and the data available from subscribing to continuous research suppliers (data is also available from this source on distribution levels and stocking levels). Less commonly available from published sources are the attitudes and policies of the organisations and their buyers. In many consumer markets, buyers' policies, their motivations and attitudes are vital factors and usually can only be accessed through interviewing (which itself is no easy task — the largest supermarket chains have daily requests for help in research).

Some industrial markets have minimal distribution structures — at least larger consumers are supplied directly by manufacturers and main importers. However, in other businesses (eg building and agriculture), distribution networks are comparable to consumer goods' retailing and a few are Byzantine in complexity (eg the motor trade). Generally, distribution in industrial markets is less well documented compared with consumer market equivalents. Nethertheless, relevant data may be found in published reports of specific markets. Also the networks themselves may be the subject of reports (eg there are several available reports on builders' merchants) although this type of information may not relate to a specific market or product of interest. Attitude data is also unlikely to be obtainable in industrial markets.

Source references for distribution and retailing are given in Chapters 6 and 7.

PRODUCTS

Examples of relevant product information for market research include:

■   Analysis of available products — their specifications.
■   How the products meet consumer needs and their satisfaction levels.
■   Packaging.
■   Product life cycle.
■   Product innovation.
■   Analysis of new product launches.
■   New product development:
    —Gap analysis
    —Consumer acceptance
    —Tracking new product launches.

An analysis of the products available in a market, including packaging methods, is often an extension of market analysis. In consumer markets, published reports, purchased data from providers of continuous research and the marketing and general press are all important sources of published information which can be collected through desk research. The same sources may also provide data on new product launches and their successes or failures. In industrial markets reports may also be available but a major source, less relevant in consumer markets, is through collecting trade promotional literature. Sources of this type are covered in Chapter 8.

Attitude data on products, as on suppliers, is far less likely to be available from desk research and new product development data on market 'gaps' (in function, sector or need fulfilment), consumer acceptance of a new product and post-launch tracking data, can only come from primary research. However, an *ad hoc* project in new product development may include a useful desk research element to provide an analysis of the established products or to show the fate of other new launches in the same market.

PRICING

Pricing data may cover:

■ Current price levels.
■ Retail margins.
■ Price trends.
■ Consumer sensitivity to prices.
■ Testing alternate prices for a specific product.

The current price levels in consumer markets are mainly well documented in published reports, data from continuous research suppliers, press features and specialised publications (eg *Which*[2]) and advertising. The same sources may also be used to plot price trends over time and in some cases the data, together with reliable information on volume sales at corresponding times, may be adequate to construct a simple price/volume model of the market. The reports may also provide data on retail margins but as this is variable and subject to negotiation, general data (eg . . . typical margins are 25 per cent for the retailer . . .) may be of very limited value.

In some industrial markets, pricing data comparable to the sources for consumer markets may be available. This is most likely to be found in the business to business office markets (there are business equivalents to Which). In other industrial markets, pricing is less accessible from published sources. List prices may be available but often mean very little since discounts are always negotiated between supplier and customer. Average prices may be obtainable from sources such as *Business Monitor*[1] or in markets dominated by imports from foreign trade statistics but at best this sort of data gives only an initial indication and only primary research may provide detailed price data. The same is true of consumer attitudes to prices and particularly in research where the objective is to test possible price levels, often in combination with product concepts which vary in other ways.

Areas such as this clearly lie outside the scope of desk research. Sources for pricing data are provided in Chapters 6 and 8.

PLANNING FIELDWORK

The types of information discussed above are all substantive — they provide data of direct relevance to meeting the objectives of market research projects. Desk research also has an important role in planning primary research. At least in quantitative fieldwork, the accuracy and value of the fieldwork data is dependant on using a controlled and representative sample. In turn this requires either a listing of the individuals making up the population or at least knowing its key parameters against which a sample can be compared.

In consumer markets secondary sources are used particularly to set sample quotas in terms of basic demographics — eg sex, age, social grade, marital status etc and these may be for the national, regional or even local populations. Sources of such demographic data may be based on government statistics (eg from *Annual Abstract of Statistics*[3], *Social Trends*[4] and various population census data) or other research (eg the *National Readership Survey*[5]). In practice, adequate data may be accessible in various publications which draw statistical data from several sources — the *Marketing Pocket Book*[6] is just one (and a modestly priced) example of this type of source. Sampling in consumer research is based commonly on area classifications using data from or samples generated by organisations specialising in this area (eg *CACI*[7]), while full random sampling may involve using electoral registers.

Desk research also has an important role in planning industrial research fieldwork. In this case the 'population' is the companies in a market or industries. Full listings of companies may be generated from various directories (eg *Kompass*[8]) or the database equivalents (*Kompass* data can be obtained as a tailored printout). However, for reasons mentioned in the previous chapter — Pareto's 80:20 rule — a random sample of companies in a market will not be satisfactory. Instead we may wish to include all the top ten companies, a quarter of companies in the next band and a much smaller percentage of the tail end of the industry.

To achieve this in practice we need companies listed by size (or at least in size bands). This may be possible from directories but in some markets it may be necessary to carry out quite extensive desk research, using a variety of sources, before selecting the sample.

EVALUATING THE INFORMATION

All that is published is not necessarily accurate. It may even be quite untrue. However, print conveys authority and there is a common tendency to take published data, uncritically, at face value. Computer databases possibly legitimise dubious data to an even greater degree. The thorough researcher should therefore attempt, wherever possible, to evaluate the accuracy and reliability of secondary data. This is not always easy and each piece of information must be judged on its own merits. However, there are some general principles to apply.

■ **Go to the original source.** Reports and statistics, particularly those published by the government, may be summarised in in the general press. Such reports, however, often omit any mention of qualifications made by the original producers of the data (sampling error in opinion polls is a very good example of this — the press report will focus on the 2 per cent lead of a party but not mention that the claimed accuracy level is +/− 2.5 per cent). This also applies to some international data but the problems of going to the original source in this case may be quite formidable.

■ **How was the original data collected?** All secondary data ultimately depends on primary research. Wherever possible the methodology should be understood. Was the data from some sort of census (of population or industrial establishments) and what level of coverage was achieved? In the case of government statistics the *Guide To Official Statistics*[9] is worth using as part of any evaluation. Often published statistics are based on samples and further details such as sample size, coverage and methods of selection should be sought out, particularly if the accuracy of the data is critical.

It may be necessary to contact the originators of the data before making a final judgement.

■ **If possible cross check from more than one source.** It may be possible to obtain the same data from two independent sources (make sure they are independent) — eg trade association and government sources. The data can be compared for consistency and differences reconciled.

Comments on the need to evaluate data, understandably, may be unwelcome. Having spent days tracking down some elusive statistics, the last thing you want is for the accuracy to be in doubt or to have to spend more time in evaluation. Obviously some sense of proportion is needed; within a restricted timetable you cannot fully evaluate every piece of secondary data and a judgement has to be made based on what level of accuracy is actually needed — what actions will follow from having the information. Often a low level of accuracy is, in practice, quite sufficient. Market size is a case in point. If your company is considering entering a new market as a niche supplier it probably does not really matter whether the overall market is worth £45 million or £65 million but if you are the market leader an accurate measure may be a vital factor in decision making.

4

FINDING THE INFORMATION

■

This chapter shows how to set about the process of finding market research information. Some sources are mentioned but others can be found in Chapters 5 to 9 which deal with particular information areas. We also discuss libraries and databases — the electronic equivalents of libraries — as well as making suggestions for organising desk research work.

LIBRARIES

Libraries are the traditional workplace of desk research and despite the increasing role of databases, are likely to remain a major resource for many years to come. Most researchers are likely to have a major library within an hour's journey of the office and in most, entry is free. All the major cities have a main municipal library and many have a specialised business or commercial section. A wide range of sources are held in these libraries and will generally cover most day-to-day information requirements. The big cities also have university libraries often with extensive marketing material. Business schools of universities are particularly good in this respect. Entry to these libraries may be restricted or involve a charge.

Arguably, *the* UK library is the *British Library*[10] with enormous collections of publications acquired under its copyright privileges (which in theory extends to published market research reports, some of which are very expensive to buy). The British Library has three services of particular interest to market researchers. First, there is a free access library in Chancery Lane, London, providing an extensive collection on open shelves and in archives. Secondly, the Library's centre in Wetherby loans books and documents at a modest cost and this provides access to detailed material located during desk research — it is well worth obtaining further details of this service. Lastly there is the Business Research Service which for a fee, carries out desk research for you, principally by database searching. It can be cheaper to have experts do this than attempt it yourself (again get details direct from the British Library). A charged-for service comparable to that of the British Library is offered by the *Financial Times Business Research Centre*[11]. Other libraries offer similar services and some are still prepared to provide limited information, by phone, free of charge. Accessing all these services is particularly easy by fax.

Apart from general business libraries, there are many specialists, including those run by larger trade and research bodies, some of which also offer database searching and other services. Policies vary widely on access (some are restricted to members) and charges. These facilities can be located via trade bodies (see below) or through *ASLIB*[12]. Two government departments provide valuable libraries for market research. The Central Statistical Office has a library at Newport *CSO Newport*[13] holding all CSO and many other government statistics. A helpful enquiry service is also acessible by phone. The other important government library is the Dti's *Export Marketing Information Centre*[14] — see Chapter 9 for more details.

Anyone carrying out desk research regularly will use one or two libraries frequently and learn how the collections are organised — what is on open shelves, what is archived and how material can be found through the library's own indexing. Some libraries have cuttings files arranged by industry and in other ways — these are worth consulting in any project. Also use the staff; they welcome sensible enquiries.

DATABASES

Libraries are vital but they have some disadvantages. You may have to waste an hour or more travelling, the opening hours may be restricted and not suit your timetable, and locating all they have to offer, on any subject, takes time and can be difficult. Imagine then if you had at your desk an enormous and ever growing library, always open and furthermore which had indexing in almost every possible way — you define the subject and the searching is done for you. This is now reality through on-line databases.

Databases (also referred to as 'on-line sources') are very large computer files of information, supplied by database providers and managed by 'host' companies whose business revenue comes from charges made to users. Access to such databases, no matter where in the world the files are kept, is open to anyone prepared to pay (generally on an as-you-go basis) and equipped with almost any sort of PC (personal computer) with a modem (to provide a phone link to the database) and communication software. Even from scratch, the set-up costs are, in business terms, modest (hundreds not thousands of pounds) and nearly all market researchers are likely to have access to a PC anyway (the modem link and software are very low-cost).

While undoubtably wonderful (especially to anyone who was adult in the pre-electronic era), databases are not magical. To date, at any rate, they are just filing systems, however sophisticated, and the sources of information on the databases are in nearly all cases also available in a traditional paper format. Indeed most of the data (eg from the press) originates as a publication and is then transferred to the database. The point of this is that almost everything on a database can be accessed by other means but the corollary is not true — much that is published is (as yet) not accessible through a database. A major example of this is trade journals — some are on databases but many, particularly those dealing with niche businesses, are not. This means that thorough desk research cannot as yet be limited to database searching and this is one of the drawbacks. Another is that whatever the various services tell you, skill is required to use them. Manuals and training (some of it free) are available but skill also requires experience and practice. Since the basis of charging is connection time, an inexperienced user will soon run up unnecessarily large bills. If you are likely to be an infrequent user of databases you can be caught in the trap of never having enough practice to become a competent user. It may, in these circumstances, be better to use outside experts for searches (see Chapter 10).

SOURCES OF DATA

We now describe the major types of information sources available for market research. To repeat a point already made, major sources are commonly accessible both in print (from libraries) and through databases. We deal in this section primarily with UK sources since those for overseas are covered in Chapter 9.

No market researcher will go far without using *government statistics*. The output of the Government Statistical Service is enormous although in recent years the scope has been cut back to both limit information to that which the government itself uses and to reduce the burden on providers of the raw data (eg businesses supplying statistical information). There is a source book devoted solely to government statistics — *Guide to Official Statistics*[9]. This is updated regularly and any researcher with a claim to expertise should have at least looked through this source. A simple guide is also available in the (free) catalogue of the Central Statistical Office available from Government Bookshops (HMSO). Table 4.1 lists the major statistical publications of the government. They are all discussed (and referenced) in later chapters but one to mention particularly is the *Annual Abstract of Statistics*[3]. This brings together some of the key and commonly required data and at £22.50 (1993 edition) is well worth buying. As well as the publications listed in the table, the output of the decennial population census (the first results of the 1991 census are now — in 1993 — becoming available) is a major source of demographic data (see Chapter 5). There are also other government statistics which, although not published for general sale, can be bought from the relevant departments or marketing agents (eg foreign trade statistics).

Many foreign governments and international bodies such as

TABLE 4.1 MAJOR GOVERNMENT STATISTICAL PUBLICATIONS

Publication	See Chapter
Social Trends	5
Regional Trends	5
Family Spending (Family Expenditure Survey)	5/6
Retail Prices	5
UK National Accounts	5
UK Balance of Payments	5/9
Standard Industrial Classification	6
Economic Trends	5
Business Monitor Series	6

the EEC publish statistics of comparable scope to those of the UK. These sources are discussed in Chapter 9.

Governments are by no means the only source of statistics. Sources of *other statistics* include trade associations, research bodies and many other types of organisations. The output of trade associations can be particularly relevant in market research although the involvement of these bodies in statistical data, ranges from nil to detailed analysis of the particular industry — the *SMMT*[15] for example is the major statistical source for the car and commercial vehicle markets (some of the data, however, is restricted to members). Quite apart from consulting any of their statistical publications, relevant trade and industry research bodies should be contacted in desk research projects. As with their publication output, the help given by trade associations varies widely depending on both policy towards information availability and the resources of the body — some have large staff establishments while others are run on a shoestring by honorary officers. Trade associations relevant to a particular market or industry can be located from directories such as *Directory of British Associations*[16].

Apart from via trade associations, non-government statistics can be located through general source books (see below) or those specifically covering statistics eg Clinch's *Business Statistics*[17].

There are over 30,000 *market research reports* available from their publishers on specific markets and products. Some, but only a minority, are available in libraries. Generally, reports are produced as speculative publications but some are produced initially for the purposes of the sponsoring organisation and then sold to recoup part of the research costs. Such reports can be located from a number of source books, each of which is international in scope. *Market Search*[18] lists — by product/market classification — some 18,000 reports from over 600 authors/publishers. Other source books of this type include *Marketing Surveys Index*[19], *Reports Index*[20] and *Findex*[21] — some of these listings can be accessed via on-line databases.

Published market research reports range in price from twenty pounds or so up to several thousand. Price is not necessarily an indication of depth, scope or quality; it is determined by the business strategies of report publishers. Some publishers produce only one-off or a few reports as a sideline, whilst for others this type of publication is their main business — eg *Frost & Sullivan*[22]. A number produce regular reports covering a wide field — eg *Mintel*[23], *Retail Business*[24] and *Euromonitor*[25] primarily aimed at regular subscribers although single issues can usually be bought. Some of these reports are also accessible from on-line databases. Clearly the more expensive the report, the greater the need to be sure of the coverage and data contained in it — a £25 report can be bought more or less blind but for one costing £1,000 or more, a detailed description of the contents should be sought and available from the publisher before a commitment is made. For a report at this level of cost it may be possible to look through it, at the publisher's offices, before buying. Further comments on published market research reports are made in Chapter 6.

A similar type of source to published reports is data available to subscribers to *continuous research surveys*. These offer detailed data such as sales volumes, consumer profiles by demographics and media exposure and the distribution of consumer market products. *TGI*[26] from BMRB for example covers over 500 product fields and 4000 brands. Other producers of continuous data include *AGB*[27] and *Nielsen*[28]. The costs of purchasing such data are substantial and are probably more appropriate to meeting a requirement for continuous monitoring than ad hoc research.

The *general press* is an important source in desk research and includes the 'quality' daily papers — eg *Times, Guardian, Independent* and *Telegraph* — the business press, with the *Financial Times* alone a major source of business information and news, and journals such as *Investors' Chronicle* and *The Economist*. Specific subjects may be covered in these sources as news items, whole articles or even special supplements focusing on specific industries and sectors such as those included with the *Financial Times*. The sheer volume of these publications is vast and subjects of interest can only be accessed, in library desk research, through various indexes such as *Research Index*[29] and the *Monthly Index to the Financial Times*[30]. Alternatively, and arguably more efficiently, searches can be carried out via on-line databases yielding references, summaries or full text retrieval. Key word searching of databases offers an access facility which is not possible in the published indexes, where the search has to be limited to the classifications used by the publishers (eg 'concrete reinforcement' can be directly searched for on a database but in a published directory any mentions may be included in wider 'concrete' or 'reinforcement' headings).

For industrial markets especially, the *trade press* is a particularly important data source. Every industry, trade and profession, no matter how obscure, has at least one specialised publication of its own with news and articles on its business. Some of these journals can be accessed through on-line databases but many are not covered in this way — one reason why database searching is not yet a full alternative to library research. The trade journals relevant to a particular field can be identified from a number of press guides including *BRAD*[31], *Pims*[32] and *PR Planner*[33]. Generally these journals are not included on general press indexes and may have little or no indexing of their own. Finding information of interest in a trade journal may be a matter of laboriously reading through back issues, although a shortcut may be to phone the publishers (who can be very helpful or otherwise). Another problem can be accessing the more specialised trade journals which may not be kept in public libraries. Alternatives include buying past copies from the publishers or visiting specialised libraries such as those maintained by some trade associations. A final point about trade journals is that for a particular product it may be worth searching publications covering the consuming as well as the producing industry — eg in researching flow-meters, publications covering the oil and gas industry may be as useful as journals for the instrumentation business.

To obtain information on specific companies or to build lists of organisations to be covered in subsequent interview programmes, a major type of source is *directories*. Broadly, there are two sorts: the general business directories and those covering a specific industry or type of organisation. Examples of general business directories include *Kompass*[8], *Key British Enterprises*[34] and *Kellys*[35]. These are published in several volumes with companies listed and detailed alphabetically, by location and by product with the latter usually within a classification based on the SIC — the Standard Industrial Classification. Details of companies include financial data and this is covered in more detail in Chapter 7. The company data contained in several general business directories (eg Kompass and Key British Enterprises) can be alternatively accessed via on-line databases.

Another type of general directory is *Yellow Pages*[36]. These volumes, covering specific areas, are a very good source of retail and consumer orientated businesses.

Just as each industry and trade has one or more trade journals, specialised directories are also nearly always obtainable (often the publisher of a trade journal produces a companion directory). A source book for directories is *Current British Directories*[37]. As well as for commercial organisations, specialised directories are available for the professions, local and central government and almost all other types of organisation. As a general rule, the specialised directories have a more comprehensive coverage than the relevant classifications of the general directories and may provide fuller information. Also some directories include organisations and groups not covered at all in the general directories. Specialised directories may also include general information about the particular industry including statistical analyses. The distinction between directories and yearbooks is not clear cut.

Where directories are used to build sample lists for subsequent interview, an important question is the level of coverage of the directory — are all or practically all establishments in the sector included or is the list only partial? Clearly if a sample is built up from a directory with less than full coverage it will be biased to some degree. Factors determining partial coverage of a directory may include a paid-for entry policy, some minimum size criterion or membership of a trade body. If the issue of coverage is important, the publisher may have to be contacted to clarify the position. To avoid or lessen the problem, sample lists may have to be laboriously built up from several directories.

Company financial data is ultimately derived from the published accounts of each company although may be more conveniently accessed through a source such as *Extel*[38]. Chapter 7 discusses these sources in detail.

As part of industrial market research *technical information* may be required, either as background material or to make sense of specific features of the market. Obviously technical information is a vast subject in its own right and cannot be covered in this book. The large libraries visited as part of desk research will generally have technical sections with their own indexing which can be used to locate relevant information. Also there are more on-line databases for technical than strictly marketing subjects and the required information may be sought in this way.

Finally do not forget to look under your own nose for information — *in house sources*. Other departments may have files of very useful data on markets affecting the company and this source can be extended to include what colleagues know but have not written down. This may be a very useful source of competitor information.

SOURCES OF SOURCES

In discussing each type of information source we have mentioned various source books covering the particular area (eg directories of directories). There are also some general source books which include all types of marketing information. The *UK Marketing Source Book*[39] published by The Advertising Association/ NTC is a cheap (£26 for the 1993 edition) handbook for consumer markets. A rather more expensive, but much larger and comprehensive source book is *The Source Book*[40] published by Keynote. This includes database sources and organisations providing particular types of data as well as listings of conventional publications. The British Library's *Market Research — Guide To British Library Holdings*[41] is another useful source of sources. Although these sources can be consulted in larger libraries, anyone carrying desk research regularly is likely to want to buy one or more. They are up-dated at frequent intervals (not in all cases every year).

As well as sources of sources covering the UK market, the are a number of comparable publications with an international scope. Some of these are mentioned in Chapter 9.

PLANNING THE WORK

Few would consider desk research to be an intrinsically thrilling activity but if there is any excitement it is the chance discovery of particularly relevant source. Often this comes about by chance through browsing the library shelves or background reading and an element of the unplanned has a value in desk research. However, in general you will only find what you seek and if you look in the right places. As in all activities, therefore, planning should precede action.

All serious research should start with defined objectives and a listing of the information needed to meet this objective. This was discussed in Chapter 2 and desk research starts with this initial plan. Also, before visiting a library or phoning trade associations or logging onto a database, thought should be given to the types of information sources which are likely to yield the information. This can be drawn up on the basis of experience, from the suggestions in this book or any source of sources kept to hand. Some potential sources will be very likely to yield data while with others, the results may be patchy. Desk research is very much a case of diminishing returns with the data yield decreasing as time goes on — three quarters of the relevant information will often be found in the first quarter of the time spent searching. Almost every researcher will be under time constraint either to meet a deadline or to keep within a budget and it is, therefore, important to consult all the sources with a high probability of yielding information first and cover the remaining sources as a secondary priority (and possibly not completely). To make most use of time in a library, go in with a plan of the sources to be consulted even though you expect to add to this or amend it on the basis of initial work.

In on-line database searching a plan — a search strategy — is even more important since, without this, expensive and fruitless computer time will be incurred — see Chapter 10.

Having located relevant data it must be recorded. Often this is best done by photocopying and in most libraries this service is available for a modest cost (subject to some copyright restrictions). However, very long or very short material is probably better précised in note form. Notes from separate sources on separate pages allow subsequent sorting of the data when a report is prepared. Always but always record the source of the data — the publication and date and if it is a secondary report of another document, record the primary source. These sources can then be given in a report and/or back-checked. It is also good practice to keep a record of all sources consulted, including those which are not fruitful. In a larger project this will help ensure the search is as comprehensive as possible and may provide useful lessons for subsequent projects. Eventually most researchers build up, however informally, their own lists of key sources.

In Chapter 3 we mentioned the need to validate desk research data. Wherever possible this should be done at the time the data is first consulted — eg notes taken of the basis of the original primary data (sample size etc), a search for the original documentation in the case of secondary reports and consideration of the need for and sources of cross-checking.

BEYOND DESK RESEARCH

In Chapter 2, desk research (secondary data) and fieldwork (primary data) were treated as quite separate and distinct activities. However, in practice, this separation is not so clear cut. Following up an article in a trade journal by phoning the editor is an obvious next step, but, arguably, falls into the primary branch of data collection. Other examples of such extensions to desk research include: contacting the author of an article (rather than the publisher), phoning or visiting trade associations and interviewing other 'expert' respondents. Sometimes the link between desk research and such fieldwork is two way — a published source leads to a personal contact and, in turn, the contact suggests additional published sources. Useful information can also be obtained by observation — eg retail store visits to check what is in stock and pricing.

Contacts and interviews of the type suggested provide *overviews* rather than data which is aggregated (eg as is usual with consumer interviews). A formal questionnaire is not required for this type of work but prior planning is essential to obtain the most from the contacts made. A checklist of areas you want to cover with each respondent is the best approach even though it may not be followed in sequence or in every detail.

5

THE MARKETING ENVIRONMENT

■

As we mentioned in Chapter 3, markets do not exist in isolation. Every market links to others, to the whole economy and, ultimately, to the whole world. This marketing environment includes the economy, demographic, social and lifestyle factors and the industrial structure. This chapter discusses these and signposts some of the desk research sources available.

USES OF MARKETING ENVIRONMENT DATA

The link between the wider national and international economy and a specific market is well understood. A general downturn in the economy coupled with rising unemployment and low consumer confidence has a directly negative effect on most consumer markets and, by a knock-on effect, on industrial sectors. High interest rates effect capital investment levels and, therefore, the demand for industrial plant and equipment. Fluctuating exchange rates may lead to cheapening imports or make it harder to sell into export markets. And so on. Other macro factors similarly affect or shape markets. Demographic trends can stimulate markets — for example, the UK is an ageing population and although this creates problems, it also offers marketing opportunities in services and products targeted at older age groups. Other social changes also form part of the marketing environment; rising crime is a social menace but underpins the market for security products such as alarms and locks. The direct impact of demographic and social factors is usually on consumer rather than industrial markets (although here too there are knock-on effects). The equivalent macro factor in industrial markets is the industrial structure of the national, European and other overseas markets. The market for printers' inks, for example, will be linked to the structure of both the printing and printing machinery industries.

In most market research studies and particularly those analysing the structure of a market, some reference to aspects of the wider marketing environment is both appropriate and useful, with perhaps a brief section identifying the macro factors which appear to affect the market. However, do not overdo this. All markets in one way or another are linked to the wider economy and every market research report does not require an analysis of the UK (or other) economy over the last decade. It is probably enough to note that the market for the product has grown or shrunk in sympathy with the whole economy or, if this is not the case, to highlight briefly this fact and quantify the variance ('. . . the market appears relatively recession-proof with positive growth evident despite the general economic recession of 1991 and 1992' . . .). Also avoid amateur economic punditry. Economics is a complex, sophisticated and controversial discipline and most market researchers are not intellectually equipped to make a sensible contribution. It is usually enough to limit any comments to noting the major trends which appear relevant to the particular market, without attempting to explain them. This danger of straying into and over-simplifying established disciplines also applies to other aspects of the marketing environment. Demographics may only have two basic variables but it is still a subject with its own body of theory and knowledge which can easily be misused in ignorance.

It is only a short step from providing background information on the marketing environment and identifying the key macro factors, to statistical modelling. A simple correlation model of brick demand to an index of construction industry activity is an example. Such models not only increase understanding of the dynamics of a market, but may provide the basis for forecasting. However, forecasting of this type requires not only historic data of the independent (construction industry activity) and dependant (sales of bricks) variables, but also a reliable forward projection of the independant variable. Such forecasts of the macro economy (or other elements making up the marketing environment) may be available but their reliability and accuracy may be another matter. Economic forecasts, by even the best qualified, may not measure up to actual events.

The marketing environment and associated macro factors are not only a source of direct or indirect substantive information but are also often an important element in planning primary research. In consumer research, for example, quota sampling is quite common; the sample is selected so that in important characteristics, it mirrors the known profile of the population being covered in the survey. This requires relevant demographic and similar data to be available — eg age structure, socio-economic groupings, marital status etc and usually at both regional or even local as well as national level. All such demographic data is readily available. In industrial market research, comparable data may be the numbers and size distribution of the businesses making up the market. Again this sort of data can be accessed through initial desk research.

THE ECONOMY

The Government Statistical Service is the original source for nearly all data on the economy. Various government publications provide economic data for both the immediate period and past time series. Key economic variables include gross national product and income, industrial output overall and by sector, retail sales, employment (and unemployment), price data such as the Retail Price Index and overseas trade. This and much other data is available in a number of regular publications which are described in detail in *Guide to Official Statistics*[9].

The primary economic publications of the Government Statistical Service include the annual 'Blue Book' — *United Kingdom National Accounts*[42] which provides detailed analyses of national income including by sector, and, for overseas trade data, the 'Pink Book' — *United Kingdom Balance of Payments*[43]. However, for most market research purposes the detail and complexity of these sources is too much and it is often more convenient to consult summary publications which bring together the key economic indicators — eg *Economic Trends*[44] and particularly the annual supplement rather than the monthly volumes. Even that general compendium *The Annual Abstract of Statistics*[3], or, for more current data *Monthly Digest of Statistics*[45] may have adequate economic data to meet the needs of a market research project. If economic indicators are needed at regional level the data will probably be available in *Regional Trends*[46].

In the next chapter we will refer to the government's *Business Monitor*[1] series as a data source for specific markets, but these publications are also sources for the wider economic background. The Annual Census Of Production Summary Tables — PA 1002 with an overall summary of production and output and Overseas Trade Analysed In Terms Of Industries — MQ 10 — for imports and exports, provide data at industry level if a sector analysis is appropriate. Statistical data for a specific sector or industry may also be available from non-government sources and particularly trade associations. In a few sectors, including the motor industry and steel, the data from trade bodies is more detailed than is contained in the government publications.

As well as in conventional published form, some of the key economic data from the Government Statistical Service is available on-line from the CSO Databank (*Central Statistics Office*[47]) via a number of hosts including WEFA — (see also Chapter 10).

The wider economy is reported, interpreted and analysed continually in the press. Publications such as *The Financial Times*[48] and *The Economist*[49] provide background understanding of economic affairs and are often a sufficient source of economic statistics. Specific topics can be searched for through the various indexes mentioned in Chapter 4 or via on-line databases.

The press is also a first source to go to for economic forecasts, which may be required for use in models linking market trends to wider economic variables. The ultimate source of such forecasts (which you may need to consult directly), include the government (eg Treasury forecasts as set out in the Budget), specialist organisations such as *The Henley Centre for Forecasting*[50] and *The London Business School*[51] and international bodies eg *OECD*[52]. However prestigious the authors, the forecasts produced from these sources are by no means infallible.

A final general economic subject to mention is price levels. With levels of inflation running at up to double percentage figures over the last decade, trends, over a number of years, in market size, company turnover and profits etc obtained at current values, need adjusting for price changes. For consumer markets the Retail Price Index will usually be appropriate and is fully detailed in the Government Statistical Service's *Retail Prices*[53] and is summarised in the more general government publications. For industrial markets, the relevant *Business Monitor*[1] for the sector provides more specific price indices.

DEMOGRAPHIC DATA

For convenience only, in this section the scope of demographic data is limited to the basic facts on population — eg births, deaths, age structure, occupation and distribution by area. The major source of this data is the Office of Population, Censuses and Surveys' decennial *Census of Population*[54] and first results from the 1991 Census are now (1993) becoming available. Census data is of considerable interest to market researchers and is the basis of both survey planning (eg setting quotas) and segmenting the population for marketing purposes including by the proprietary geo-demographic systems such as Mosaic and Pinpoint. Such is the importance of Census data, the Market Research Society, in conjunction with NTC, have published *An Introductory Guide to the 1991 Census*[55].

For most day-to-day purposes, demographic data is probably easier taken from more general government publications including *Social Trends*[4] and the *Annual Abstract of Statistics*[3] rather than the census data itself. Much of the key data is also abstracted in other publications providing marketing statistics — eg The Advertising Association/NTC's annual *Marketing Pocket Book*[6], a cheap publication well worth having on your desk. Such sources are in many respects easier to use than the government publications and may provide demographic analyses that are not directly available from the 'official' sources — eg population profiles by ITV region. Demographic data is also included in these publications from sources such as major readership surveys and TGI.

Demographic data is available from on-line databases — eg *Harvest*[56] — although for many purposes consulting a desk-top publication such as the Marketing Pocket Book is probably both easier and more convenient, as well as much cheaper.

SOCIAL AND LIFESTYLE DATA

The boundary between demographic and social and lifestyle data is vague or artificial. Rather than 'simple' population data, the term social and lifestyle covers aspects such as behaviour (eg marriage and divorce, crime), household spending patterns, patterns of employment, leisure activities, transport, housing and ownership of products. Government publications providing statistics in these categories include the general sources such as *Social Trends*[4] and *The Annual Abstract of Statistics*[3]. Two more specialised government sources are the *Family Expenditure Survey*[57] and the *General Household Survey*[58]. Both are regular or continuous surveys carried out by government agencies and reported in one or more publications which are issued annually or every few years. The Family Expenditure Survey was originally carried out to provide a basis for the Retail Price Index but the range of data on spending patterns, with the various related analyses, makes the survey of wide interest. Each year, the General Household Survey covers both standard topics (eg housing, migration patterns, employment, education, family structure) and ad hoc subjects to meet current information needs of government departments. The government or its agencies and special commissions also publish, from time to time, reports on specific social issues or problems and these may be relevant to a particular market research project.

Social and lifestyle data is also available in marketing compendiums such as the *Marketing Pocket Book*[6] and a companion NTC publication the *Lifestyle Pocket Book*[59] (also cheap). There are as well a number of established published reports on lifestyle which are revised from time to time. The costs of these are all in the £100–200 range. Titles include: *Lifestyle Trends in the UK*[60], *Targeting Adults*[61] and *Consumer Market Factfile*[62]. Information on lifestyle is also accessible through databases — eg *Harvest*[56]. The press also provides factual data and commentary on social and lifestyle trends. Specialised studies carried out by academic sociologists may occasionally be relevant but generally those useful for marketing purposes can be picked up in the general press (where the summary of the research may be in sufficient detail).

INDUSTRIAL STRUCTURE

Industrial structure is in industrial or business to business market research the equivalent of demographic and social and lifestyle data. An understanding of the structure of the industry, of which a market is part, is commonly needed either to provide a meaningful analysis or as a basis for primary research sampling and other aspects of survey planning. Typical data sought may include the number of establishments and their distribution by size or area. The overall output of an industry with trends over time, levels of imports and exports, employment patterns and investment levels may also be relevant to the objectives of a particular project. Industrial structure is documented in detail by the Government Statistical Service and particularly in the *Business Monitor*[1] series. Relevant Business Monitor publications include:

- **PA 1002** — this annual summary volume of the annual census of production shows by industry, the number of enterprises, sales and output, purchases, value added, employment and other statistics.
- **MQ 10** — a quarterly analysis of imports and exports by industry.
- **PA 1003** — an analysis of UK businesses by size (turnover breaks), industry classification and geography (county and region).

Summary industrial structure data is also available in general government publications such as the *Annual Abstract Of Statistics*[3] and *Regional Trends*[46].

In the sources mentioned, industries are classified by the Standard Industrial Classification (SIC), a system which has recently been modified to bring it into line with a common EEC classification. This is set out in *Standard Industrial Classification of Economic Activities*[63]. SIC is widely used not only in government statistics — trade directory publishers such as Kompass and Dun & Bradstreet use it as the basis of their own product classifications. Other systems to be noted include that used for imports and exports and the classification of businesses for VAT purposes.

Apart from government sources on industrial structure, there are the company databases maintained by providers of information such as Dun & Bradstreet and ICC. These are based on the accounts of companies and are published in reports and directories as well as being accessible as on-line databases. More on this subject in Chapter 7. Analysis of the structure of individual industries is also available from the enormous range of published market research reports, but this type of source is discussed in the next chapter. Finally, the press and especially the more specialist business papers and journals such as the *Financial Times*[48], *Investors' Chronicle*[64] and the *Economist*[49] also provide, in articles or special supplements, analysis of industrial structure. A summary of press coverage of particular industries is provided by the industry 'cards' published by *McCarthy*[65] and available in some libraries.

6

MARKET ANALYSIS

Probably the most common type of research project attempted through desk research is a general analysis of a particular market. Information of this sort is often used in business planning including market entry or diversification strategies. Specific topics covered in market analysis, for both consumer and industrial markets, may include; market size and segmentation, growth (or decline) of the market and the factors (the dynamics) underlying these changes, profiles of the consumers, suppliers and their position in the market and the distribution network. This chapter shows how to find published sources of information in these areas.

MARKET REPORTS

By far the easiest way of acquiring information on a market is to buy a published report covering your area of interest and, with 30,000 or more such reports available, there is quite a good chance that there is at least one publication more or less matching your particular requirements. Even the cheaper reports are usually based on an extensive research programme, including specially commissioned primary research as well as desk research. A full analysis of a market, covering at least most of the topics mentioned above, is usually provided. If such a report is available and meets your particular needs, you will obviously seriously consider its purchase and offset the price against the cost of time you would otherwise spend on desk and possibly primary research.

Methods of locating reports were mentioned in Chapter 4. A good starting point is to use *Market Search*[18] and this can be supplemented by similar source books or by accessing on-line databases of published reports (publishers/database providers include — *Marketing Surveys Index*[19], *Reports Index*[20] and *Findex*[21]).

Some report publishers offer a very wide range of titles across either consumer or industrial markets and it may be worth being on their mailing lists to receive complete lists of their titles and news of new reports. A few publishers market their reports in monthly publications with each issue containing reviews of three or four different markets (largely consumer rather than industrial or business markets). Examples of such serial publications include *Mintel*[23], *Market Research GB*[66] and *Retail Business*[24]. Annual subscriptions for these publications are quite substantial (hundreds of pounds upwards) and will only be worth considering if your interests regularly span a range of the markets covered over a year. However, single issues can usually also be bought and although a premium is charged, this still provides relatively low-cost access to data on your market. Some of these publications can also be accessed via on-line databases, but at costs comparable to the charges for the hard copy. There is, however, a virtually free route to these sources — some libraries are subscribers to one or more of them and, therefore, you can effectively have access to the data at no charge at all. If the subject of your research is likely to be covered in the serial reports — most consumer markets are — consulting them should be part of your desk research routine and particularly if you can see them for free (you are not allowed to photocopy them).

Other publishers also offer relatively low price information with title lists spanning a very wide range of markets and subjects, but marketed as single issue rather than subscription publications. *Keynote*[67] is an example of this type of publication. The titles available from Keynote cover mainly consumer markets (some business to business as well) and typically the contents of each comprise: industry structure, customer profile, major players and market size with sector analysis. At under £200 per report, they are good value, but again some libraries buy the reports and, therefore, provide free access to the data. Checking out whether Keynote has covered your subject should also be routine.

An interesting new product from Keynote is their Briefing series. Each title is a four-page summary providing the basic facts on the market. Each costs around £50 and could offer a cheap source of the key data on a market. To date (late 1993), only a limited number of titles are available, but the publisher may roll out the series to offer wider market coverage.

Another series of relatively low-priced reports (and available in libraries), including both industrial and consumer markets, is *ICC Business Ratio Reports*[68] published by the same group as for the Keynote titles. An overview of the market is provided in the reports but the focus is a financial review of the companies involved and, therefore, this is not a source to provide a complete market analysis (see also comments in the next chapter).

A specialist publisher of reports on industrial markets is *Frost & Sullivan*[22]. These reports provide full and detailed analysis including of markets for technical products and services. The geographical scope is international rather than UK and may cover the whole World, Europe or North America (Frost & Sullivan is a US company). Prices of titles are substantial (typically over £1000) and their value depends on the match between the report coverage and your specific needs.

As well as the publishers mentioned, reports are available from many others and these can be identified from the source books mentioned earlier. Costs range from the almost nominal to the very expensive and, at least for publications in the higher price bands, you need to know what you will be getting before ordering. Generally the publisher will have a descriptive brochure and table of contents available and this can be supplemented by phone enquiries. For the most expensive publications, you can expect to be able to see and look through the report at the publisher's offices before commitment and perhaps to have access to the report writers for follow-up queries as an after-sale service. Whether the asking price represents value for money depends on the match to your specific requirements and ultimately on the value attached to the research project you are carrying out.

Although the volume and range of published reports is enormous, you may find that no report closely matches your specific area of interest. It may be that your focus is on a narrow niche market that is only covered, in passing, in reports on the wider industry or market of which it forms part (eg paving bricks may be only cursorily mentioned in a report on the whole brick market). Alternatively, your interest may cut across recognised markets (eg the market for domestic hot water systems may be covered in reports on boilers, central heating, pipes, plumbers' merchants and plumbing services) or be a composite of several (eg leisure centres may be covered in reports on the market for separate sports). In such cases you need to define and identify the markets which in one way or another relate to your own interest and find the reports that are available and what information they offer. You then have to make a judgement whether the partial information available through the reports offers value for money.

In discussing published reports we have considered sources which more or less offer complete market analyses. We now turn to collecting information on the topics which make up a market analysis — market size, trends, suppliers etc.

SIZING MARKETS

Market size is the total value of the goods or services supplied into the particular market over a year — the amount spent by consumers. Related but different concepts are manufacturers' sales and the potential market. Manufacturers' sales are the output of relevant products by domestic suppliers operating in the market and therefore include exports (sales to overseas customers) but exclude any imports coming into the market. As we shall discuss shortly, market size can be calculated by combining the separate data for manufacturers' sales, exports (subtracting) and imports (adding).

Potential market is a rather vaguer concept and is the theoretical value of the market if all possible consumers bought the product to the maximum possible level of consumption. Calculating (often this is little more than a guess) the value of the potential market in this way, can show the growth potential of the market and may be an input into forecasts of future market size.

Market size is also of course different from the value of sales by a particular company (eg your own) to the market, unless there is a 100 per cent monopoly situation. The link between the sales of a particular supplier and the value of the whole market is market share and obviously if you know the value of a supplier's sales and have an estimate of market share you can calculate market size. Occasionally this is a route to arriving at the market size estimate but, more importantly, it is a cross check — if given the estimate of market size, the known sales of a major supplier indicate an unrealistic market share (too big or too small) the estimate will need reconsidering.

Market size may be expressed in value or quantity (tonnes, gallons, units etc). A value estimate is nearly always required and the quantity equivalent may be useful. An important issue in value estimates is at what point in the distribution chain does the estimate apply. In consumer markets and some industrial markets the prices paid by final consumers are higher than that received by the manufacturer or major importer — the difference being the retail/distributor mark-up or margins. It is important to establish and define for any market size estimate whether the values are at retail or manufacturers' level. If your estimates are at manufacturers' prices (eg via Business Monitor — see below) and you require the retail value, you will have to make an adjustment based on an estimate of the margins ruling in the particular market. This problem arises in all consumer markets but is not an issue in some industrial markets, where supply is direct from manufacturer/ importer to final consumer and with no distribution structure intervening.

Now to sources and methods for estimating market size. A first step is to use one of the source books which list data sources by market or industry; several were mentioned in Chapter 4 including *UK Marketing Source Book*[39] and *The Source Book*[40]. These will identify sources which may include market size estimates (and other aspects of market analyses). There will be an overlap with searches of sources for published reports and obviously the full market analysis report will include estimates of market size. Other types of sources likely to be identified in general source books include statistics from government (see below for the major government source for market size) and other bodies, including trade associations, periodicals covering the particular market and databases. In some cases it will be explicit that the source provides market size estimates, but in others the reference will have to be followed up to find the precise nature of the data.

Compendiums of marketing data include estimates of the value of various markets and more detail may be found by going to any original sources given. Similarly there are publications available which bring together estimates of market size and other key data across a wide range of markets. Examples include *Market Assessment of Top Markets*[69] and a companion volume of market forecasts, *Market Forecasts*[70] — both cover several hundred markets, mainly but not wholly in the consumer field. Another publication to mention is *Market Size Digest*[71], a Mintel publication in monthly issues bought on a year's subscription — single issue purchase may be negotiable.

The general, business and trade press may be all potential sources of market size or other market analysis data. The general and business press can be searched through the indexes or via databases as described in Chapter 4. Specific estimates of market size are more likely to be mentioned in passing and for this reason may be difficult to locate specifically. Where such estimates are found, the sources, if quoted, should be followed up; where none are given, be sceptical — they may be no more than the writer's guess. Trade journals are also a fruitful source of market size and other useful data. As mentioned in Chapter 4, trade journal searching may involve going straight into the publication since some are not covered in the general indexes or databases. The relevant publications can be identified from the various press guides (see Chapter 4) or general source books. A shortcut to data in trade journals may be to phone the editor or other publishing staff.

Source books or specialist directories (eg *Directory of British Associations*[16]) will also identify trade associations, research bodies etc covering the particular market. These should be contacted as potential sources of published (or unpublished) data on market size; though their ability and willingness to assist is very variable.

The various producers of continuous market research — eg *TGI*[26] — have data available for market sizing. As explained earlier, these organisations are geared to providing long-term access to their databases at relatively high costs and are unlikely to be economic sources for one off ad hoc projects. However, some of the data is indirectly accessible through other publications — eg *Mintel*[23] reports include TGI data.

The final source of market size data to discuss is arguably *the* key data source in at least industrial markets — *Business Monitor*[1]. Business Monitors are a series of publications, but the largest group are the Production Monitors and it is these which are used in market size estimates. Each Monitor covers a specific industry or product grouping based on the SIC classification and provides, in separate tables, figures for manufacturers' sales, imports and exports by detailed product breakdown. There is also data on the number of establishments involved in the industry as well as price changes. At one time the Production Monitors were published quarterly but now most come out annually and provide figures for full years only. The data in the Monitors can be used to arrive at market size estimates at both industry and detailed product level (find the relevant SICs from *Standard Industrial Classification of Economic Activities*[63] then go to the appropriate Monitor); the basic calculation being to add imports to manufacturers' sales and subtract exports. Long time series are available from the Monitors and, therefore, past changes in market size can be plotted and perhaps used as one input in making future forecasts.

In some of the Monitors, a difficulty has been that the product classification for manufacturers' sales is different to that used for imports and exports (which originate via Customs & Excise) and various re-grouping and estimating work has been necessary to bring the data together for market size estimates. This problem is now to be solved through bringing the product classifications into a common EEC framework and in future the three sets of figures (manufacturers' sales, imports and exports) will be compatible. The EEC and the single market has, however, raised new problems for Business Monitor. Inter-EEC trade (eg sales by a British manufacturer to a French manufacturer and vice versa) are no longer part of 'foreign' trade. With no customs barriers and no import/export documentation to prepare, imports from and exports to other EEC markets are no longer captured as part of Customs & Excise foreign trade statistics. The problem will be overcome by incorporating data from VAT returns (which record inter-EEC sales and purchases) into the Monitor tables, but the exact format of this is as yet (late 1993) not finalised. This and other queries on the Monitors can be sorted out by contacting the very helpful enquiry service run from Newport (*CSO Newport*[13]).

Business Monitor statistics can be used to segment market size by product breakdown. However, other sources will have to be found for segmentation by consumer group, geography etc since these are not documented in the Monitors.

As well as being a component of market size, import and export statistics may have a value in their own right in a market research project. They can, for example, show the breakdown of UK exports of a product by destination and this may be an indicator of export opportunities. Similarly import data by country of origin may be useful — in some markets virtually every product is imported and, therefore, imports will equate to market size. Summary import and export data is available in a number of publications of the Government Statistical Service including as part of the Business Monitor Series (eg MQ 10 — Overseas Trade Analysed In Terms Of Industries). The product and market coverage in these sources is broad, but detailed product analyses of import and export data can be purchased from commercial agencies marketing Customs & Excise data — eg *Tradstat*[72]. Changes in the statistics because of the Single Market are also, at time of writing, being made in this area with, in future, inter-EEC figures originating from VAT returns.

PROBLEMS IN MARKET SIZING

It has so far been assumed that estimating market size is simply a matter of finding the source which gives the figures for the market of interest. However, research is often not that simple. None of the available data may cover your specific market. For example, engineers' cutting tools can be made by a variety of techniques one of which is based on powder metallurgy, and in one project it was this type of tool that was of specific interest. Statistics on engineers' cutting tools are available but those made by powder metallurgy are not broken out. In another project the market being analysed was motor mechanics' tools distributed by 'wagon jobbing' (garage to garage selling from vans). The Monitor data classifies the market by the type of hand tool (spanners, screwdrivers etc) rather than who uses them (garage mechanics) or who sells them (via vans). In some cases these sorts of problems cannot be overcome through desk research alone — the market size you want simply is not documented in any published form and only primary research will provide the answer. However, reasonable estimates can be arrived at with some ingenuity and by bringing together data from disparate sources. Approaches to consider are top-down and bottom-up estimates, aggregation of suppliers and linked markets.

Market boundaries are quite arbitrary. We can see any as either the sum of its constituent parts or as a sub division of a larger market. Top-down estimates take the larger market — eg all engineers' tools or all hand tools — and quantifies that market. Since Business Monitor covers all industry, you can arrive from this source at one or more quantified markets which include the grouping of specific interest. Having obtained data on this larger market, the task is now to make estimates of what proportion of the total is accounted for by the narrower product field. This may be arrived at from press and trade journal research, the known sales of leading suppliers and possibly the informed opinion of experts (see Chapter 4).

Bottom-up estimates divide the market of interest into its product elements and seek data for these smaller classifications. Quite possibly, this approach will lead to estimates for part, but not all, of the market and the gaps can be filled by making reasonable estimates in the same way that the larger market was split into the smaller area of interest.

Markets are made up of the sales of suppliers and if these (or the largest) can be estimated, then the market size is calculable. In some cases, the sales of one supplier known to dominate the market can provide an adequate basis for estimating the whole, although there is often the problem that the turnover of a leading supplier covers sales into a number of markets.

Finally, an estimate of market size might be made from statistics of consuming or otherwise linked markets. For example, if the objective is to estimate the quantity of plastics used as packaging in the soft drinks industry, the method could be to obtain data on volume sales of the drinks and estimates of packaging method (cans, glass, plastic). Together with some estimate of pack unit sizes, a figure for plastic bottles for soft drinks can then be calculated which in turn can be used with estimated quantities of plastic in each bottle (if necessary by getting hold of samples) to arrive at an estimate of the required market size in volume.

These and other approaches which may be valid in particular cases, can be used with some ingenuity to arrive at estimates of size in most markets. Of course they are estimates and probably ones whose level of accuracy can only be guessed. However, the point has already been made (see Chapter 3) that low levels of accuracy may meet the purpose of the research. Also, where desk research is part of a wider project, initial estimates might be a starting point for refinement through primary research. With experience of researching a range of markets it is often possible to recognise an estimate that is grossly out; there is some sense of scale likely depending on the nature of the market. Niche industrial markets, for example, are seldom worth much more than a few million pounds or so, while standard grocery product groups may top £100 million. The table below illustrates some scales of market size.

TABLE 6.I   THE SCALE OF UK MARKET SIZES

Market	£Million
Beer	12000
Books	1200
Power Tools (retail)	119
Pizzas (retail)	50
Baths (DIY, retail)	15
Medicated Footcare	4

Sources: various reports

OTHER MARKET ANALYSES DATA

Apart from market size, other market analysis data includes trends, consumer profiles, suppliers and distribution. Generally, the sources mentioned for market size are equally relevant to these other aspects of market analyses and in practice the researcher identifies all the relevant data as he or she goes through the sources.

Quantifying changes in market size is normally covered in establishing the current value (eg Business Monitor provides past time series figures). Understanding why the changes have occurred is rather different and is more likely to come from the more discursive sources such as the general and trade press. It helps, however, to think of the factors which could possibly have led to change and in any market these may include:

■ **Macro factors.** These are the economic, demographic and other factors, discussed in the previous chapter, and which may be the main dynamic of market change.

■ **Product innovation.** Innovation can stimulate markets and may even create the market (eg personal computers). At least major product changes will be reported in the trade press.

■ **Changes in the consuming market.** These include changes in taste and fashion, needs and structure. In consumer markets structural changes take a long time, eg the dominance of owner-occupation through the housing changes from the 1950s to the 1970s. In industrial markets structural change can be rapid through takeover, reorganisation or the fall-out from recession (eg in only five years in the 1980s the number of drop-forging establishments fell dramatically). At least sudden changes will make the trade news and long-term factors will be the subject of articles.

■ **Legislation.** Some markets are shaped by legislation and changing regulations. Emergency lighting is one example where extending the legal requirements for the products has led to short-term upsurges in demand. Again the trade press is the best source; any legislation likely to affect the market will certainly be reported.

Consumer profiling in consumer markets is generally available from the published reports on the market or from suppliers of continuous data. These sources may also be quoted in the general and trade press. In industrial markets, structure is usually in terms of the numbers, sizes and area distribution of the businesses making up the consuming market. The Business Monitors and other sources mentioned in Chapter 5 are the starting point for this type of data.

Suppliers to a market can be identified from directories as well as the trade and general press and the latter may also provide estimates of suppliers' shares of markets. The various general marketing compendiums may also give suppliers or brand shares (in consumer markets the brands are usually of primary interest). Another approach is by profiling the supplier companies from financial data and press mentions. These sources are discussed at length in the next chapter. One problem of this route, however, is that companies often make a range of products and sometimes for radically different markets. The turnover of Ferodo is, for example, indicative of its position in the brake lining market since that is the principal business of that company, but ICI markets such a wide range of chemicals and other products that its turnover alone is little guide to its position in any chemical market.

The marketing strategies and tactics of leading players in a market are often the subject of press reports and, for consumer markets, in the marketing press especially — *Marketing*[73] and *Marketing Week*[74]. Advertising activities by sector are analysed in a number of publications including the Advertising Association's annual *Advertising Statistics Yearbook*[75] and data from *MEAL*[76].

Information on a distribution network may be sought in the trade press, in specialist reports (located as for market reports), from suppliers of continuous research data or, as for primary suppliers, by company profiling.

7

COMPANY INFORMATION

■

Markets are organised around companies, or in few areas, around other types of business organisation. Companies are the suppliers to a market; as manufacturers, major importers or at the various levels in a distribution chain. In industrial or business to business markets, companies are also the main consumption units. In market research, information about companies is a common requirement including assessment of market shares, evaluatation of competitors and, in industrial markets, the understanding of major customers. Information on companies is also required in planning fieldwork (primary research) for industrial and business to business research; all the companies in a market may have to be listed as a sampling frame and a sample selected using information on the companies such as turnover or turnover bands, number of employees and location.

This chapter describes the information on companies which can be obtained through desk research and how to find it. At the end of the chapter some other types of organisations apart from companies are briefly mentioned.

COMPANY ORGANISATION

A basic understanding of the various forms of companies in the UK is required by a market researcher. The most common type of business organisation (or 'enterprise') is the limited (ltd) or public limited (plc) company. Unlimited companies exist but they are a rarity. In some professions partnerships predominate (in some eg solicitors, only partnerships or sole proprietorships are allowed). Unlike limited and public limited companies, the accounts of unlimited companies and partnerships are not accessible or in the public domain (this may be precisely why a company is unlimited).

The essential difference between limited and public limited companies is that the latter (plcs) may invite the public to subscribe for their shares while limited companies may not. Plcs must also have to have a share capital of at least £50,000; so while they are above the micro business level they need not be large — many limited companies are larger than some of the smaller plcs. There are also some other technical differences between plcs and limited companies but these are of little interest here except to mention that there are some accounts' disclosure differences which will be discussed shortly. Many people confuse plcs with quoted companies — companies whose shares are traded on a recognised market such as the London Stock Exchange. All quoted companies have to be plcs but the converse is not true — there are many plcs that are unquoted.

Companies can own the shares of other companies (usually the shares of limited but sometimes public limited companies) and where a controlling interest is held, the company is a subsidiary of the company owning the shares. Sometimes within a group structure the shareholding company is referred to as the parent and the others are termed the operating companies. Generally, it is such operating companies which trade in markets; buying, manufacturing and selling. Market research information is usually needed at operating company level. Sometimes companies are divided into divisions. This is a vague term and unlike a subsidiary company, a division has no legal existence. From a researcher's point of view, divisions are unhelpful since separate accounts are not produced. To complicate matters further a group may also own a number of dormant companies and these may have the same name as a division — dormant companies by definition do not trade and although accounts have to be prepared these are a few lines in length and, for market research purposes, worthless. To either establish the ownership of a subsidiary or identify the structure of a group of linked companies, the best source is *Who Owns Whom*[77] — one of the many directories published by Dun & Bradstreet.

A final term in business organisation to mention is 'establishment'. An establishment is a business activity carried on at one specific site. This may also be the sole site of the whole company or of a subsidiary or operating company. However, the site may be just one of several locations where the company carries on its business. In industrial and business to business market research, sampling is often required on an establishment rather than company level, since the former is commonly defined as the consuming unit.

IDENTIFYING COMPANIES

Directories of various sorts are used to identify and list supplier companies in a particular market or locate basic information about a particular company. As mentioned in Chapter 4, directories fall into two broad groups; the general business directory and those focusing on a particular industry or activity.

Sooner or later most market researchers are likely to have one or more of the general business directories in their office. The major UK coverage directories of this sort include *Kompass*[8], *Key British Enterprises*[34] and *Kellys*[35]. These directories list businesses by product classification (either SIC or related to it) as well as alphabetically and by geographic area. Various other details may also be given including financial data and classification by turnover or employment band (both of which are particularly relevant in sampling for industrial research). There is obviously considerable overlap between these directories and few would want to own all three. However, each is better or more convenient depending on the task and it is well worth being familiar with all of them.

As well as in conventional published form, the data from Kompass and Key British Enterprises is accessible from on-line databases (and such data may be more up to date than the directory entry). As well as immediacy, on-line access also allows listings to be tailored to meet a specific purpose — eg all businesses within one or more trade classifications, listed in order, by turnover grouping and by location within turnover band. The publishers will also, for a charge, prepare such listings for you (or you can order on-line and have it delivered next day). The databases can also be obtained in diskette and similar form and this also allows computer manipulation on your own hardware.

The general directories list companies rather than establishments (although in some cases a clear distinction is not always made). In industrial or business to business primary research, sampling often needs to be at establishment level. *Market Location*[78] maintains a database of industrial establishments with detailed information on each. Tailored lists to meet specific requirements can be ordered from this company. Another source of establishment listing is *Yellow Pages*[36] — each volume covers a specific area and can be a good source, in particular for the more 'retail' trades. A practical problem with *Yellow Pages* is that several or even all volumes are needed to build a national sample and duplication is a problem. Special printouts from the *Yellow Pages*' database can overcome this.

The detail and value of directories covering a particular industry vary considerably. Some provide no more data than can be obtained from the general directories but others are both more comprehensive and give greater detail about the companies making up the industry. The types of equipment and plant in operation at a company may for example be given. Specialised trade directories also often list establishments as well as companies. Directories of this sort can be located through *Current British Directories*[37] or from some of the source books previously mentioned.

FINANCIAL INFORMATION ON COMPANIES

Financial information available on individual companies includes turnover, expenditure under various headings, profit (from profit and loss accounts) and details of what is owned and owed (from balance sheets). Turnover is generally the financial data of most interest in market research and may be used in estimating the size of a market (by aggregating the turnovers of the major suppliers) or calculating market shares. A difficulty already mentioned is that an individual company often sells into a number of different markets and total turnover is seldom split by market (export sales are separately identified).

Apart from turnover, other financial data may be required in preparing a report on a particular market. The profits made by the players in a market are obviously of considerable interest in projects to plan diversification or market entry. Profits can be shown in value or in various ratios — eg profit : turnover and profit : assets (return on investment). Various other indicators of financial health can also be used including those relating assets and liabilities. There is some line between including financial data as part of a wider market research study and rather more detailed financial analysis. Specialised skills and expertise are needed for full financial analysis and most market researchers are not competent to do the work. Also, as will be mentioned shortly, financial analysis of specific industries and sectors can be bought off the shelf and may far better meet needs for financial analysis than anything likely to be produced ad hoc by a market researcher.

At least some financial data can be obtained on all companies registered in England and Wales or in Scotland (under separate arrangements). The basis of this data is the legal requirement on companies to prepare annual reports and accounts to recognised standards and file them at a Government agency — Companies House — where they are available for inspection by any enquirer. At one time enforcement of the filing requirement was lax but in recent years has become far more rigorous with stiff penalties for non-compliance. This may not be welcome to accountants and company secretaries but is of benefit to researchers who are now less likely to be frustrated in searches for up to date accounts data.

The general requirement is for a company to file a full set of its audited accounts and directors' report with Companies House. Concessions are made for companies classified as 'small' or 'medium' — see Table 7.1 for definitions — which may file abbreviated accounts only. In the case of 'small' companies the abbreviated accounts are a shortened balance sheet only, while 'medium' companies need file only an abbreviated profit and loss account without turnover disclosure but with a full balance sheet and directors' report. Since, in research projects, turnover is usually of prime interest, these concessions to smaller companies are not helpful. However, since the concessions do not apply to a public limited company or any company which is a member of a group containing a public company (or to various types of financial companies), full accounts are available for the operating companies of most larger groups. Furthermore, while small and medium companies can file abbreviated accounts they may choose to return full accounts since preparing abbreviated accounts is an extra chore (full accounts are still required for the shareholders). All this means that in most markets full accounts should be available for at least the major players.

TABLE 7.I   SMALL AND MEDIUM COMPANIES FOR FINANCIAL DISCLOSURE PURPOSES

	Small Companies	Medium Companies
Any two of the following:		
Turnover	< £2m	< £8m
Balance Sheet Total	Not more than £975,000	Not more than £3.9m
Employees	Not more than 50	Not more than 250

Companies House keeps filed accounts (for companies registered in England and Wales — there are separate arrangements for Scottish companies) on microfiche and copies of these can be obtained by visiting either the main Cardiff or the London offices. The data can also be bought by post or, for premium charges, obtained by fax. However, for most purposes it is easier to use an agent to do the work for you; their charges are quite modest. One such agent is *Circare*[79] who will not only supply microfiches of companies but for a few pounds per company, prepare a short summary of key data (eg turnover, profits and balance sheet totals) from several years' accounts. This may meet requirements without having to find your way through the full microfiched accounts.

Another approach to collecting company accounts is via organisations whose business is to collect and analyse this sort of data. The *ICC Group*[80], for example, maintains a database of all British (including Scottish) companies with revised accounts added to files as they become available at Companies House. Accounts of individual companies can be obtained from ICC including by on-line access to the database. ICC also prepares reports — eg ICC Business Ratio Reports (£195 each in 1993) — analysing the financial performance of companies in an industry or sector, including comparisons, by ratios, across the companies making up the sector. Other organisations including *Dun & Bradstreet*[81] and *Infocheck*[82] maintain comparable databases and can supply financial details (particularly geared to credit checking purposes but the reports are also of wider interest) of individual companies including by on-line access.

The reports and accounts of *quoted* companies can usually be obtained by simply asking for them (contact the company secretary's department); they are in the public domain and in no way secret. The reports and accounts of large quoted companies are often substantial publications and may contain comments and analysis of the company's businesses. Of course, these are written for a purpose (eg to sugar the pill for shareholders) and may be neither dispassionate nor objective.

Another source of financial data on quoted companies is *Extel*[38] who produce their well known cards summarising current and past accounts for quoted (and some leading unquoted) companies. The cards can be ordered from Extel and are also available in some libraries (photocopying not allowed). The financial results of quoted companies are also reported and analysed in the press.

OTHER COMPANY INFORMATION

Apart from 'hard' financial data, other information about companies operating in a market is of considerable interest to a market researcher. New product launches, strategies for market entry, production resources and marketing methods are all aspects of companies which may be relevant to a particular research project. News and analyses of companies are provided in every issue of the 'quality' national press and particularly the *Financial Times*[48] and the weekly *Investors Chronicle*[64]. Reports on individual companies can be located through the indexes or on-line searches mentioned in Chapter 4. The marketing press — *Marketing*[73] and *Marketing Week*[74] cover companies in consumer markets and often analyse the marketing strategies and tactics used by the companies in particular sectors. News and press comments on major companies are also abstracted and summarised by *McCarthy Information*[65] and is available on McCarthy Cards (some libraries subscribe to this service) or through on-line access.

Specialised trade journals also contain detailed reports and articles on companies in their own industries and at the operating company level and this type of source may be more fruitful than the general press. The problems of searching through trade journals have already been mentioned.

Local press can also be searched for reports on companies and particularly for those which are dominant employers in their areas. However, this level of detail is seldom worth pursuing as part of a broad market research project and the need would have to be exceptional to plough through the reports, many of which will be in the 'gold watch for 40 years loyal service' vein. Also back copies of local papers are generally only available in the libraries of the immediate area.

Information and publications put out by the companies themselves should not be ignored. The reports accompanying the accounts of companies have already been mentioned. Other forms of self publicity include general brochures, product literature, marketing mailings and media advertising. Obviously the information is presented to put the company in the best possible light and must be treated with caution. However, it is often possible, from these sources, to gain an insight into the marketing methods of companies. Collecting this sort of literature may be as simple as writing and asking for it (after all, it is not secret), visiting trade exhibitions (literature on all major companies in a market can be picked up at once) or by more ingenuous methods, some of which might be considered unethical, so they are not described here.

Analysis of companies' (or more strictly brand) advertising expenditure in the media (but not 'below the line') can be obtained from *MEAL*[76].

OTHER ORGANISATIONS

As well as companies, other organisations active in particular markets include central government and its agencies, local authorities, other public bodies and various types of trade associations. By and large, sources of information are similar or the same as for companies. All types of public bodies for example publish annual reports and accounts and these are generally freely available and accessible in many libraries. Accounts of local authorities — in some markets either suppliers or major consumers — are collated and analysed in publications of *CIPFA*[83]. The press, including trade journals, is also a source for news of these various bodies.

8

PRODUCT INFORMATION

■

Companies compete in markets with products. Part of a market research brief, therefore, is often to analyse what is available in the market place and much of the required information can be collected through desk research or allied methods.

This is a short chapter; not because the subject is unimportant but to avoid wearying the reader through repetition. Many of the sources mentioned for market analysis and company information are also relevant for products. Indeed product information usually falls out of these other types of project and to regard product research separately is, to an extent, artificial.

IDENTIFYING AVAILABLE PRODUCTS

Trade directories include product listings, often with details of their features, branding and sometimes pricing. Similarly, the trade press includes product reviews and news of new launches. Even advertising in these sources can provide useful information.

In some markets there are publications which specialise in reviewing available products with feature and price comparisons. The most well known of such publications is *Which*[2] covering from time to time, most consumer markets. There are also many magazines of the Which format covering specific product groups, particularly leisure and hobby markets. There are as well trade sources such as *Glass's Car Guide*[84]. In some business-to-business markets there are also product review publications eg *What to Buy For Business*[85].

Quite another approach to building knowledge of retail products is store visiting: observing what is on offer and possibly buying samples. Arguably this is moving outside strict desk research and there is a continuity with 'mystery shopping' exercises (where researchers pose and act as shoppers) which are strictly aspects of primary research.

In markets where mail order is strong, the catalogues are the shop windows for products and usually include short informative product feature descriptions. Mail order is not only established in consumer markets but has made inroads into some industrial and business to business markets eg computer peripherals, electronic components and safety equipment.

COLLECTING TECHNICAL INFORMATION

In many industrial markets, the product ranges are made to explicit and rigorously monitored standards. They may also compete on features or through offering different technologies. Product standard data is available from the authorities who establish them — either industry-specific eg oil industry safety standards or those of such as the *BSI*[86]. However, market researchers' interest is usually in the features which differentiate products and brands, and product literature and catalogues are nearly always available from the manufacturers in the particular market — they are a standard marketing tool. In consumer markets, product literature is often less comprehensive, although this is not the case with complex products such as cars, cameras and electronic equipment, with literature aimed at retailers if not final consumers.

In industrial markets, the most direct method of collecting product literature is by requesting it by phone or letter. It is seldom not forthcoming (obviously if the supplier believes you to be a potential customer the response will be with greater alacrity), but a by-product may be calls from sales staff following up their leads. In some cases, researchers may use mild subterfuge; the reader must consider the ethics of this. Also for practical reasons it may not be credible to pretend that you represent a potential customer — eg in markets for large capital equipment where all the potential buyers are well known. As mentioned in the last chapter, exhibitions and trade fairs are also opportunities to collect literature from a wide range of suppliers. Possibly, you may also be able to talk to suppliers' representatives on their stands. These events, however, are infrequent and may not fit into a research timetable.

PRICES

Sources providing details of the products on offer will also often give matching price data. This may be actual retail prices (eg Which and similar consumer sources as well as some advertising) but in other markets 'list' prices may be given. Depending on the market, such list prices may provide a basis for calculating retail prices through applying known discount rates and retailers' margins. In a few markets the 'list' price may be the actual price — eg publishing. Mail order businesses obviously sell at the advertised list prices.

Problems in obtaining pricing data can be quite considerable in many industrial markets. 'List' prices, if given at all, may have only a very loose connection to what is actually paid or prices are simply not published and are a matter of haggling between seller and buyer. In such cases, collecting any data on prices may be outside the scope of desk research.

PRODUCT LAUNCHES

Desk research is generally considered to have no value in new product development and clearly it has no role in establishing consumer reaction to your new product; the most common research requirement in new product development. However, the fate of other product launches in your market may provide useful guidance to your own strategy and especially where the new product is only marginally differentiated.

Previous new product launches are often well documented.

Sources to consult include the trade and marketing press and all the sources discussed in Chapter 6. Through desk research, therefore, information can be collected on the products launched in the past, the marketing backing given to the launch, possibly the intended strategy behind it and quite often, in at least consumer markets, the sales/market share obtained and the length of time over which this was achieved. Information of this type may suggest how your own product should be launched and possibly may contribute to an assessment of its potential.

Conventional marketing wisdom has it that most new products fail — certainly a lot do. There may be more to learn from past failures than from an analysis of success. Information on failures is harder to find than reports of success. Launches are accompanied by much publicity and any success will not be hidden. Failure is a different matter and little may be available unless the disaster is of mammoth proportions. Generally the products just disappear from view. Finding information on failed new products is therefore often harder than collecting data on their launches, but the sources are likely to be the same — the marketing and general press, market research reports etc.

9

OVERSEAS DESK RESEARCH

■

Up to this point the focus of the book has been desk research for UK markets. With the advent of the single EEC market, businesses are looking to wider markets than the home territory, so market researchers will increasingly seek international data. By the end of the decade it may be as parochial to limit analyses to the UK alone as it is currently to restrict research to only one English region. Desk research is particularly cost effective in multi-country research. There are extensive sources available and the cost savings compared to primary research are even greater than in UK-only projects.

A difficulty in writing about overseas research is that at least a chapter, if not a book, could be written on researching every developed economy. For practical reasons the emphasis is selective and largely restricted to Europe as a whole (particularly the EEC) and the US.

In international research, a working knowledge of several of the main languages is a considerable asset. However, the monoglot researcher need not despair; many international reports are written in English or have English summaries. Also the main sources of statistics often have English headings and even where not, the use of standard classifications, coupled with a dictionary, enables identification and comprehension of relevant data. Real language problems can arise in searching foreign press and trade journals but even in this case English abstracts may be available and accessible via on-line databases.

LIBRARIES AND INFORMATION CENTRES

All the main libraries with a good range of material for UK desk research are likely to have sources for overseas research and the researcher's regular library is a sensible starting point for international data. There is an important specialised library which should be included in any major international project — the Dti's *Export Marketing Information Centre*[14] in Victoria Street, London. As well as an open access library, the centre provides guidance and information about overseas markets and maintains a product database. You can just turn up at the library but it is better to discuss your needs in a preliminary phone call. Also, seek help from the library staff thus gaining the most benefit from your time there. The data sources on overseas markets, including statistical material, available in this centre, are considerable.

Other Dti information points which are worth contacting for overseas research include the regional Dti offices, and for Europe the EC Country desks, which can provide advice and guidance over the phone. Initial contact with the Dti can be made through phoning the *Dti Hotline*[87]. A Dti database — *Spearhead*[88] is also available although this primarily offers information on the institutional framework of the EEC. Other various (free) publications can be obtained from the Dti including a publication listing sources of advice.

The Dti offers financial assistance for export market research although principally to help cover the cost of research involving fieldwork rather than desk research. Details can be obtained from the Dti or from the scheme administrators; the Association of British Chambers Of Commerce — *ABCC*[89]. Where a project is likely to involve any fieldwork, the availability of a grant should be discussed at an early stage with the Dti or ABCC.

The EEC Commission itself is proactive in offering information about the single market through a network of *European Information Centres*[90]. There is a centre in each UK region based in a 'host' organisation. Much advice is offered including market intelligence.

SOURCES OF SOURCES

There are quite a few publications listing and indexing sources of market and business information for international and particularly European markets. These, to varying degrees, list sources across countries (eg for the whole EEC), for specific countries and by market, product or subject. These publications are available in the larger libraries and should be used early on in any serious international desk research project.

Sources of sources for European markets include Keynote's *The Guide*[91] covering organisations and on-line databases as well as conventional publications, Euromonitor's *European Directory of Marketing Information Sources*[92] and *European Directory of Non-Official Statistics*[93], Industrial Aid's *Published Data On European Industry Markets*[94] (particularly relevant for industrial markets) and London Business School's *Guide To European Market Information*[95]. There is of course considerable overlap between these guides.

There are also source books with a worldwide coverage, including Europe. The *Directory of International Sources of Business Information*[96] by Sarah Ball is worth consulting with coverage of information providers, country data, and industry sources. There is a particular emphasis on on-line databases which provide international data. An extensive listing of international statistical sources is provided by Gale Research's two volume *Statistical Sources*[97]. This is a US publication and is particularly thorough for US statistical sources, including those from the many government departments, but it also includes sources for the rest of the world.

Two international source books for the press are *Benn's Media Directory International*[98] covering newspapers and periodicals and Euromonitor's *European Directory of Trade and Business Journals*[99]. In earlier chapters, trade associations have been mentioned as potentially important sources of information on the industries and markets they cover. A source book for European bodies is CBD Research's *Directory of European Industrial and Trade Associations*[100]. Incidentally, a UK trade body may be a source of international as well as domestic information: possibly they have carried out research of their own on the international market of interest.

INTERNATIONAL MARKET REPORTS

As discussed in Chapter 4, the easiest way of acquiring information on a market is to find a published report covering your own area of interest or at least partially matching your needs. With thousands available there is a reasonable chance of finding at least one. Published reports cover overseas as well as domestic markets and many reports have a multi-country scope. The EEC and the main member countries, the US and Far East markets are all well covered. The US market in particular is extensively researched for off-the-shelf reports. The sources for locating reports, mentioned in Chapter 4 — *Market Search*[18], *Marketing Surveys Index*[19], *Reports Index*[20] and *Findex*[21] — all cover international as well as UK reports. Another directory with a specifically European consumer market scope is Euromonitor's *European Directory Of Consumer Market Reports And Surveys*[101]. The country coverage in these sources is indicated in each report entry. As for UK reports, the costs of publications vary widely and for the dearer ones careful judgement of their value must be made before commitment.

A number of UK publishers offer relatively modest priced, serial reports covering European markets and often complementing a similar UK title. Generally these cover consumer rather than industrial or business to business markets and are sold on annual subscriptions, although single issue purchase can often be negotiated. Some of these reports are also available (for free) in libraries. Examples of these types of reports include *European Product And Market Reports*[102] from the Data Group, *Marketing In Europe*[103] and *European Retail*[104] from the EIU, *Market Research Europe*[105] from Euromonitor and publications from *Mintel*[23] and *Keynote*[67]. Some of these reports, or data from them, can also be accessed from on-line databases.

As well as reports published regularly through the year, with a number of products covered in each issue, there are annual reports bringing together market or socio-economic data but again mainly relevant to consumer markets. One of the cheapest publications of this type is NTC's *European Marketing Pocket Book*[106]. Euromonitor also have some pan-European annuals — *European Marketing Data and Statistics*[107], *European Compendium Of Marketing Information*[108] and *Consumer Europe*[109]. A recently published (1993) market compendium is *European Market Share Reporter*[110] claiming coverage of 1500 product markets arranged in SIC order.

Generally, industrial markets are not as well served by publishers of relatively cheap international reports. However, there is a very wide range of one-off reports which can be located in the report source books. The US market for industrial and technical products is particularly well covered. *Frost & Sullivan*[22] are a leading publisher of this type of report and their list includes international as well as US reports — costs are relatively high; in the thousands rather than hundreds of pounds. Abstracts of these reports are available on-line. A similar publisher is *Predicast*[111].

The marketing and advertising backing for products across Europe and worldwide is covered in a number of regular reports including *European Advertising Marketing and Media*[112] from Euromonitor, and from NTC *European Advertising and Media Forecast*[113] (quarterly) and *World Advertising Expenditure*[114].

The availability of macro economic statistics from major international bodies and national governments will be referred to shortly. It is appropriate to mention that there are many publications bringing this type of data together in a convenient form. Two such publishers are the *Economist Intelligence Unit*[115] and *OECD*[52].

THE PRESS

The UK general and business press carry news, reports and extended analyses of international markets as well as overseas company information. There are also frequent overviews of individual countries. Specific titles worth consulting include the *Financial Times*[48] and *The Economist*[49]. As explained previously, specific articles in these and the rest of the press are best located through indexes such as *Research Index*[29] or via on-line database searches. Some trade journals also have an international scope and should be considered, particularly when researching industrial markets.

The national press and trade journals in other countries are also good potential information sources but there are practical barriers limiting access. There is the problem of accessibility; most of the foreign press is simply not available in local libraries or possibly anywhere in the UK. There is also the problem of language to overcome. Some access is possible through on-line databases with the bonus of English abstracts. In some industries a trade body will have its own specialist library keeping foreign press reports and articles; this should be established through making contact with the relevant trade body as a routine element of a major desk research project.

The language problem obviously does not arise for US markets and at least the major business publications and trade journals can be found within the UK. The US press is also well indexed or included in on-line databases — eg Predicast's *Index of Articles Published*[116].

INTERNATIONAL STATISTICS

Extensive international statistical sources are available and relevant for data on the marketing environment (economic, demographic and social statistics as discussed in Chapter 5), industries and individual markets. Providers of such statistics include not only virtually all national governments but also several international bodies and these are considered first.

The EEC is a major collector, analyst and publisher of statistics. The office responsible for this is *Eurostat*[117] based in Luxembourg. Some of the major regular publications available include:

■   *Basics Statistics Of The Community* (annual) — a compendium comparable to the UK's Annual Abstract Of Statistics

■   *Demographic Statistics* (annual) — self-explanatory

■   *Eurostat Review* (annual) and *European Economy* (quarterly) — main economic indicators for the Community and member states

■   *Family Budgets* (occasional) — an analysis of household expenditure comparable to the UK Family Expenditure Survey

■   *External Trade Statistics Yearbook* — imports and exports of the Community.

■ *Industrial Production* (quarterly) and *Industry Statistics Year-book* — statistical data on the output of sectors and industries

These publications are only a small part of Eurostat's full range and details can be obtained from the organisation's offices. Alternatively, there is an independent guide available, *Eurostat Index*[118], now in its fifth edition (1992) and providing a keyword index to the statistical series available from Eurostat. Also included are details of on-line access to Eurostat data. Eurostat maintains its own database — Cronos Eurostat — and this is accessible through several hosts (eg WEFA — see Chapter 10).

The United Nations is also a major publisher of international statistics; but in this case with a worldwide scope. The UN has its own statistics office in Geneva although it is probably easier to contact the UK office — *United Nations Information Centre*[119]. A catalogue of UN statistical publications is available free of charge. Some UN publications of potential value in international research include:

■ *Statistical Yearbook* — economic and social data
■ *World Statistics In Brief*
■ *Industrial Statistics Yearbook*
■ *World Economic Survey*
■ *Economic Survey Of Europe*

Another international body regularly publishing statistical data is the Organisation For Economic Co-operation And Development — *OECD*[52]. Again a free catalogue is available. Titles include:

■ *Indicators of Industrial Activities* — in member countries, by sector
■ *Main Economic Indicators* — covering 25 countries
■ *National Accounts of OECD Countries*
■ *Statistics of Foreign Trade*

The OECD's publications can be obtained through government bookshops in the UK, as well as direct from the organisation's Paris offices.

The USA, the world's largest economy, is well documented in State and Federal government statistics. These are the responsibility of many agencies but one of the most important is the *Bureau of The Census*[120] of the Department of Commerce. The *Statistical Abstract of The US*[121] is the Bureau's annual compendium, comparable to the UK Annual Abstract, and is a first source for US data. The Bureau is also responsible for a five year census of manufacturing — *Census of Manufacturing*[122] which provides an analysis by SIC of manufacturing output; the level of detail is excellent but may be several years out of date. There are also comparable censuses of the service industry and transport activities. The Bureau of Census also carries out a population census — as in the UK, every ten years — with data published in a wide variety of forms down to neighbourhood level. Other offices of the Department of Commerce are responsible for US foreign trade statistics and can provide detailed analysis of imports and exports by product groupings. Forecasts for industrial sectors are published in *US Industrial Outlook*[123]. The full range of industrial statistics from the department is described in *Guide to Federal Data Sources on Manufacturing*[124].

The statistical output of the Department of Commerce is likely to meet many market research requirements but other departments of the Federal government as well as State governments also produce and publish extensive data. A general source guide to all US government statistics is published by the Congressional Information Service — *American Statistics Index*[125]. Gale's general statistics source book — *Statistical Sources*[97] — is also a very good guide.

Every government in the world produces statistics for their own country and at least the major developed economies have a range of data comparable to that produced by the UK or US governments. Access can, however, be a practical problem; even the specialist libraries such as the Export Marketing Information Centre keep only a fraction of what is available worldwide. On-line database searching may, however, locate national government statistics and the coverage by this route continues to expand rapidly. Another alternative is to carry out desk research in the countries of interest and where a programme of visit interviews is planned as part of the whole research project, this may be the best approach.

OVERSEAS COMPANY INFORMATION

Companies operating in overseas markets can be identified, as in the UK, through directories. A visit to a major or specialist library will show what is available for the countries of interest. There are a number of publishers with international ranges of country directories and perhaps the best known is *Kompass*[8]. Each national volume or set of Kompass is to a common format, with the trade classifications to a similar system and, therefore, the language problems are minimised. Another publisher offering a wide range of national trade directories is *Dun & Bradstreet*[81]. The Business Reference Collection of Dun & Bradstreet spans all the European countries, Asia and the US (which alone is covered by forty or so different directories including the Million Dollar Directory Series and the various Moody volumes — though these have a more financial than market focus). Another major US directory is *Thomas Register of American Manufacturers*[126] — this consists of twenty or so volumes with product and service supplier breakdowns as well as company profiles.

As well as national directories, there are publications with an international coverage, eg — Graham & Trotman's *Major Companies of Europe*[127]. However, for many market research purposes this type of directory seldom offers enough detail and there are directories of specific trades for nearly every country. If a full listing of suppliers of a particular product is required, this type of source can be far better than the general directories but accessing such publications can be a serious practical problem. For some industries there are international directories (often English language) and where available and relevant these should be used in building lists of suppliers or profiling selected companies.

The databases used by leading directory publishers are available increasingly on-line (eg Kompass On-Line) and this often provides the most effective method of generating lists of companies, to defined criteria, for use in interviewing programmes.

To varying degrees, financial information from the accounts of companies is available in most developed countries. However, the requirements for disclosure and filing — the legal basis for the availability of this type of data — vary widely as do the legal forms of company organisation. In many countries registration and filing of accounts is at a local level and there is no centralised access point such as the UK's Companies House. The position in the EEC and other European countries is described in detail in Gale's *Sourceguide to European Company Information*[128]. In the US, company disclosure is based on the '10k' report — financial and other details which companies must file with the Securities Exchange Commission and make available, on request, to any enquirer.

For most purposes in a desk research project, the only practical route to obtaining financial data on overseas companies is to use the services of companies specialising in company data — *Extel*[38], *ICC*[80] and *Jordans*[129] or access their databases on-line. All these offer international services and should be contacted to discuss specific needs.

10

ON-LINE DATABASES

■

On-line databases were briefly covered in Chapter 4 and sources available on-line have been mentioned, in passing, throughout the book. Using on-line databases is now central to desk research; if you carry out this sort of work regularly, this data source is seen increasingly as essential.

There are problems with on-line databases and these are considered in this chapter, but for many market researchers, the advantages are overwhelming. First and foremost there is the sheer scale of accessible data — there are gaps, but much of the key material is there and effectively in one place: your own desk. Immediate access also offers convenience and efficiency. Time is not wasted in travelling to libraries and once in the database, retrieval is far faster than from library shelves. This enables deadlines to be met which, without on-line access, are quite impossible. It is quite feasible to put together a market structure report in a matter of hours rather than the days needed by traditional desk research. On-line data is also almost always up to date; the entries in a current-year conventional directory, for example, are generally at least one year and maybe two or more years out of date, while the database from which the directory is printed is probably updated daily and accessible on-line.

This chapter covers the structure of the database industry, what is accessible and, practically, how to get into on-line research.

DATABASE PROVIDERS AND HOSTS

The provision of on-line data is an industry with some major information and communication companies involved. The basic

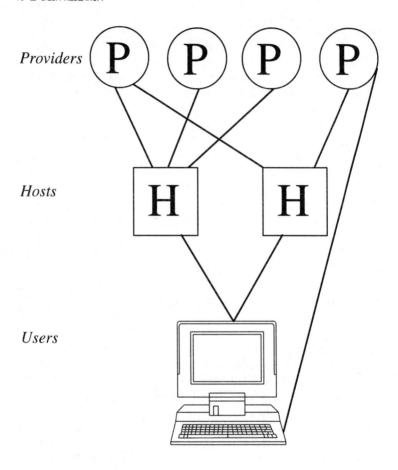

Providers

Hosts

Users

FIGURE 10.1   DATABASE PROVIDERS, HOSTS AND USERS

structure is as Figure 10.1 and consists of 'providers', 'hosts' and 'users' — you and me — linked through the phone network.

Providers of information are the 'authors' — they collect the data, in some cases specifically to offer it on-line but often to publish it primarily in paper form. Usually anything on a database is also available in hard copy from the provider. Examples of providers include directory publishers such as Kompass, market research publishers such as Mintel, Keynote and Frost & Sullivan and producers of statistical data, including the UK government and Eurostat (for EEC statistics). There are also providers offering abstracts or, increasingly, the full text, of newspapers and journals — eg Reuter Textline. Database providers may keep the data on their own computers or input it into hosts' datafiles via magnetic tape or through a phone link.

Hosts are effectively the distributors of on-line data. The information is on databases, usually several, held on their computers and it is from here that the user accesses it. You phone into the host computer, select one or more of the databases held, and by using the appropriate command language, search for and retrieve the required data. The location of the host relative to the user is of little practical consequence; the database you phone may be on the other side of town, at the other end of the country or on another continent. The providers and hosts may also be thousands of miles apart. To reduce phone charges, hosts often offer special contact arrangements which effectively provide link-ups, at local call rates, irrespective of the actual distances — eg a user in Manchester can access Data-Star's Swiss computer by dialling local area phone codes.

Hosts typically hold data from a number of data providers and the user can therefore access the data from several in one connection. To complicate the picture, some providers may supply data via more than one host and some also offer the user direct connection without going through a host (effectively the provider is its own host). A few providers can only be accessed directly. Also, some hosts as well as holding data from independent providers, maintain and offer their own databases.

A final aspect of the structure to mention is the 'gateway' concept. Some hosts allow users the convenience of reaching databases which are held on other companies' computers via such gateways — eg Reuter Textline via FT Profile. A practical problem of this may be that the database accessed through the gateway uses a different command language to the host's own. Even databases held by a host may operate, however, through different command languages — more about command languages later.

On-line databases are in business for profit and the hosts have a pivotal role in buying and selling data. Users buy from hosts. As a user you enter into an agreement and are typically billed monthly in arrears on a pay-as-you-go basis by the host — there are many variations in hosts' charging methods including up-front charges. In turn, providers are paid for the data by the host. The host computers also provide precise and complex accounting for billing and payment purposes. Users' charges are virtually always based on 'connect-time' — this is why efficient use of the database is vital — but may also involve charges for the amount and nature of data provided — eg by line of text. Some data is intrinsically low-cost especially if, like newspaper extracts, it is freely available in the public domain, whilst other sources (eg market research reports) are premium priced.

WHAT IS AVAILABLE FROM DATABASES

The breadth of data available on-line has been indicated in earlier chapters. It has frequently been noted that a particular source is available on-line as well as in conventional printed form. A full listing of the data which can be accessed from your own desk could and does fill several books — there are a number of specialist on-line source books available and these should be used (possibly one or more bought) by anyone planning serious database research. These include *On Line Business Sourcebook*[130] from Headland Press, two directories published by ASLIB — *On Line Business and Company Databases*[131] by Helen Parkinson and *On Line Management and Marketing Databases*[132] by Nick Parker. The Association For Information Management (ASLIB) publishes other relevant guides and a regular newsletter and also offers advice on database selection and access. Another useful database source book is the *Directory Of On Line Databases*[133] from Gale

TABLE 10.1 EXAMPLES OF ON-LINE DATABASES AND HOSTS

Database/Data Provider	Host* Providing Access
Statistics CSO CENDATA OECD Eurostat Tradstat	WEFA[134] Data-Star[135]
Press Reports FT Profile Reuter Textline Predicast Prompt	FT Profile[136] Data-Star
Market Research Reports Mintel Euromonitor Frost & Sullivan ICC Keynote Findex	FT Profile Data-Star Dialog[137]
Market Research Data TGI (BMRB)	BMRB[138]
Company Information Kompass On-Line Dun & Bradstreet Infocheck Jordan Extel McCarthy On-Line ICC	Kompass[8] Dun & Bradstreet[81] Infocheck[82] FT Profile Data-Star
Specialised Marketing Databases Harvest MAID	Mintel[23] MAID[139]

* Only one host is given for each database. In many cases the database can be accessed through more than one host and the omission of such additional hosts is not significant.

Research. This publication is particulary useful for locating US data although it has an international coverage.

As well as the specialist database guides, listings of what is available on-line are also provided in the general market research source books mentioned earlier. Keynote's *The Source Book*[40] for example has a database listing for each of the information headings covered.

Types of information available from databases include statistics, articles and news from the general and trade press, market research reports and company information. Table 10.1 lists a selection of databases under these headings and shows, for each, just one access host (there are often more than one for a particular database).

Some key statistical data provided includes UK government data from the Central Statistical Offices (CSO), US statistics from CENDATA and international series from OECD and Eurostat (EEC statistics). As shown in the table, these database providers can all be accessed from one host — WEFA. UK and other countries' import and export statistics are marketed by Tradstat whose database can be reached through *Data-Star*[135].

Not only all the major UK newspapers but also the press from all over the world are accessible through a number of important bibliographic databases including FT Profile (a host which is also an important provider in its own right) and Reuter Textline (particulary for the foreign press and major trade journals) which is also hosted by FT Profile. Another provider of trade press information is Predicast Prompt, accessible through Data-Star. Bibliographic databases such as these provide by far the most efficient route to searching the press for relevant information; even searching a few months issues of one major publication such as the Financial Times is a major task if you do not use an on-line database. News and articles, depending on the database, can be retrieved as full text or in abstract (often in English for the foreign press).

Whole market research reports or abstracts are available from on-line databases. These include the serial or series titles from Mintel, ICC Keynote and Euromonitor. Frost & Sullivan's industrial market reports are available in abstract. The Findex guide to published reports is also accessible on-line. A feature of all on-line reports is that access to the data is relatively expensive; they are premium priced (often with a hefty up-front subscription) and this should be understood before retrieval — once you have down-loaded a report you incur the costs.

Some of the providers of continuous market research make their data available on-line, again at premium prices. One example of this is BMRB's TGI (Target Group Index) which, as mentioned in Chapter 4, provides detailed analysis of product data and is accessible directly from BMRB (to subscribers only).

Company information is particularly well covered on-line with much financial data available in far greater detail than normally needed for market research purposes. Several of the major directory publishers, including Kompass for the UK and overseas and Dun & Bradstreet, market on-line databases and these can be used either for profiling specific companies or to build up lists of companies meeting specific criteria — eg products offered, size, location etc — for fieldwork sample lists. Detailed financial data from company accounts is accessible on-line from the main providers of this sort of data including ICC, Jordan, Dun & Bradstreet, Infocheck and Extel. Press reports of specific companies can be accessed from searching the general bibliographic databases or from specialists such as McCarthy On-Line. Such on-line company information sources can be used to provide the electronic equivalent of press cuttings.

The databases and hosts mentioned so far are generally marketed to, and meet the needs of, a wide range of users. Two premium priced on-line sources specifically tailored to the needs of marketing and advertising people are Harvest and MAID (Marketing Analysis and Information Database). These bring together a wide range of marketing data and offer convenient access. Most of the sources on these databases are accessible through other on-line routes.

Many of the databases mentioned above have an international scope, and in general, international market research is well covered on-line. Indeed on-line searches may provide access to data which is very difficult to obtain in conventional form.

The databases and hosts listed in Table 10.1 are illustrative examples only; the range is vast and guides mentioned earlier are substantial volumes containing little but lists of available databases. While some types of data are not yet available on-line, this must be kept in perspective. What is available and accessible from your desk is more than can be found in any one library or than would ever be located from conventional sources within any reasonable search time. If you restrict your desk research to on-line databases you will miss some types of data, but equally you will very likely cover a wider range than is possible in libraries.

Some types of data not available on-line include the more specialised trade press — journals, directories and yearbooks and particulary those covering a niche industrial market. Also not accessible are many of the one-off or short series market research reports which can only be obtained by purchase of hard copy — however, such reports can at least be located on-line (eg from Findex). Much statistical data is accessible on-line, but the coverage is as yet patchy. Surprisingly, although the CSO makes a lot of government statistical data available in this way, there are serious gaps and hard copy of some important statistics will still be needed. For some purposes statistical data which is available on-line is probably more conveniently taken from publications such as the Annual Abstract Of Statistics or one of the small compendiums. If all you need is the age and social class breakdown of the population, connecting up to a database is an overkill (and almost certainly more expensive). The same principle applies to company information — if you just need basic information on a handful of UK companies, a bound directory may be more convenient. Database over-dependency is a potential danger.

BASIC REQUIREMENTS FOR ACCESSING DATABASES

The hardware requirement for database access is a PC (personal computer); almost any will do the job and a researcher is very likely to have one for other purposes. If you are really starting from scratch the starting price is now only a few hundred pounds. You also need a modem — the piece of hardware which allows you to connect your computer, by phone, to a host. Many PCs have this facility built-in, otherwise it is a matter of buying a 'card' to fit into a computer or a separate modem unit. The cost of these add-ons is small. With a modem fitted, the computer can then be plugged into a standard phone point. Other essential hardware is a means of storing data retrieved in database searches — normally via the floppy disc drive of the PC — and a printer for hard copy; you are unlikely to have or buy a computer without these facilities.

Software is also needed to link your computer to a host's database. Often this comes as part of the initial package bought with the computer but if not, the cost of an effective system is low. This type of software is generally user friendly and, via menus, allows easy connection. The software stores the details of the databanks you buy into, including the access codes. Getting into a database can be a matter of a few keystrokes only. However, you may not want to make access too easy and wish to keep security codes to prevent frivolous or incompetent use.

With the hardware and communications software taken care of, the other major requirement is to subscribe to one or more hosts — you cannot get into databases unless you have an account with an appropriate host. Selecting which host or hosts to sign up with is the hardest part of getting started.

SELECTING HOSTS

The first point to make is that no one host will meet all possible needs. Some such as FT Profile and Data-Star can offer access to a very wide range of databases but even they are in no way comprehensive. The same applies to the databases/hosts offering services geared to marketing (eg Harvest). Choosing hosts, therefore, depends on the type of information likely to be sought. If the main requirements are to search the UK press, FT Profile would be a good choice, but for trade journal and foreign press coverage it may be necessary to supplement this with Data-Star. If it is intended to buy into market research reports, either or both these hosts should be considered. For regular access to a company database, Kompass On-Line is worth considering and if your interest is largely to access UK and overseas statistics, WEFA could be appropriate. These are only the more obvious choices.

Before deciding, think through the intended uses and compare what is on offer by consulting the database guides and contacting likely hosts. They will all have descriptive literature and in any case you will need to make preliminary contact to establish the costs entailed.

The costs and the methods of charging will also be an important factor in making an initial selection. All databases, one way or another, charge according to use but some charge solely on a pay-as-you-go basis. Others may also charge a small registration fee, or for their essential manual, or have a low minimum billing. A variant is where you have to pay for some connect time up-front and replenish this as needed — the hosts and not you take credit. Other hosts require substantial payment up-front for an annual subscription entitling you to a certain amount of access. There are other refinements to the charging system which you will need to understand before commitment, including the different pricing and possibly quite separate subscriptions to different databases accessed through one host. A further complication is that a particular database may be accessible through different databases at different charges. Finally, hosts will often offer various deals around their basic tariff including reduced rates for high volume use and cheaper rates for off-peak connection, if you are willing to work unsocial hours.

All this is very complicated and the best advice to a beginner is initially to sign up with one or two hosts which make no significant up-front charges or have no significant minimum billing commitment. Once some basic skills are learned and the value of database searching proved, you can then consider access to other databases. For general market research purposes a sensible start-up might be to sign up for FT Profile and/or Data-Star plus Kompass On-Line. However, this can be no more than a suggestion and you may well decide that others are a better initial choice.

GAINING SKILLS

There is one other essential if you are to make on-line databases effective, and that is skill in using them. In their promotional literature, hosts often say that their databases are user-friendly, easy to learn and that a beginner can be proficient in only a couple of hours. Well, they would, wouldn't they! The size of the manuals supplied to subscribers alone belie such claims. However, once you sign up, most of the hosts offer training support including free or low-cost seminars, with hands-on sessions, help desks and often initial free connect time. If you decide to go into database searching, you have to commit yourself to a learning programme. On the positive side, if your firm is paying, it is an excellent opportunity to acquire some further marketable skills.

As already mentioned, you are likely to want to use several hosts and databases and a complication is that each may require a different operating system and language. Even one host may have different languages for their various databases. There are two basic systems for accessing databases; menu or prompt driven, which are relatively self-explanatory, and those requiring you to learn a command language — these are inevitably harder to pick up initially. Menu-style operation is generally for databases providing statistics, other sorts of numeric data (eg financial), and on-line directories. Command languages are required for the bibliographic databases and it is the facility to search using keywords and other commands that make these such powerful and effective sources. The languages vary between databases but they are dialects rather than mutually foreign tongues. Once you have fluency in one, the others come quicker, although switching back and forth in one search session can be confusing.

The help needed to learn the techniques of using databases is readily available. However, as in many fields, proficiency depends on experience and experience requires frequent and regular use of the databases. Obviously, with substantial connect charges you cannot go into databases just to keep your hand in, and to be proficient you need some continuous requirement for data accessible through on-line searching. At the worst, this leads to a chicken and egg situation. You do not become proficient because your need is too small and such need as you have is not met because you lack experience in using databases. In this situation the answer may be to recognise that direct on-line searching is not for you and your organisation. This need not mean that you are denied all the benefits of databases since you can commission outside organisations to do the work for you. There are a good many suppliers offering this service including some business libraries eg *The British Library*[10], information services such as *Financial Times Business Research Centre*[11] and several of the business schools and other colleges. Of course, these organisations charge for their skilled time on top of the costs they incur in using databases but, because they are so proficient, the total cost is likely to be less than the bills run up by an unskilled user of the databases. Most providers of this service will work to an agreed budget and call a halt to their search time once this figure is reached.

Another aspect of the need to build up database searching skills is that in an organisation or department it is usually best to limit access to one or two specialists who can carry out searching on behalf of their colleagues.

USING DATABASES

Because there are a variety of database operating systems and languages, I can only cover, in this section, some of the general principles of on-line database use. The purpose is to give an indication of what is entailed rather than instructions you can practically follow — you must learn the specific systems of the hosts you subscribe to.

The most important general principle is *plan a search strategy before you log-on*. Once you are in a database the meter is running and you are incurring charges for every minute on-line. If you are sitting scratching your head and wondering what to do next, you are wasting money. To avoid this, spend time drawing up a search strategy, in writing — even if it is scrawled on a piece of scrap paper. For databases requiring a command language, your plan should include which database or databases you intend to cover (hosts such as FT Profile allow you to choose either individual databases or to search across a number), the keywords or word strings you intend to search with, and the time periods you want to include. Your plan should also be flexible. Think through the likely decision points and the alternatives you may face and if you reach a point where you are unsure what to do next, log-off and have a re-think before going back into the database. For the other sort of database — menu driven — even though they are generally easier to use, you also need a plan. If you are searching for companies on a directory database, at least make sure you have a list of them all and think through what to do where the precise name may be uncertain. If you require to generate a list of companies, make sure you have defined in advance the parameters by which the list will be selected.

With bibliographic style databases, operated by command languages, considerable thought should be given to the choice of search words or word strings. Be very careful of ambiguous terms. For example, if you are researching the mechanical spring market be wary of using 'spring' alone and without further qualification, otherwise you could end up with full text about late or wet springs and their effect on lambing! The more general the term, the greater the volume of data, but much or most of it may be irrelevant to your needs and represent wasted costs. A search for 'computer' for example will on most databases potentially fill the room with printout and virtually all of it will be useless if your interest is confined to lap-top portables with built-in printers. In this case you clearly need to add qualifying terms to 'computer'. In another market, however, where reports are likely to be few, you may need to use the widest term to find anything at all — possibly truncating the word to ensure you include all variants, eg rather than restricting the search to 'engineering' you use 'engineer*'. Another aspect of word searching which you may wish to specify is the position of the word or string in a report. As a general principle, the substance of a report (and, therefore, relevant keywords) appears early on (eg the first 50 words), while later references are often mere passing references — eg a recent article about a football club management crisis might have mentioned that Amstrad are a leading computer company, but tell you nothing useful about the computer market.

Several of the larger hosts allow you to select a specific database or cover several simultaneously. In the latter case the amount of material produced will be greater but costs will be higher. Also some of the material may be duplications; this is very much the case with press sources; it is probably enough to

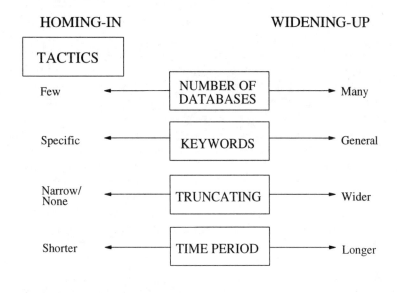

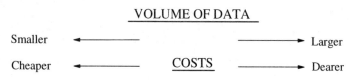

**FIGURE 10.2   HOMING-IN AND WIDENING-UP
ON-LINE SEARCHING**

have the same story in one report and not different versions from
several papers. A lot depends on the nature of the market or
product searched — with experience it may be obvious which
database is likely to produce the most useful information, and in
this case the search can, at least initially, be restricted. In other
cases it may be far from clear which source is likely to be fruitful,
and an across-database search could be the best approach. Some
hosts provide indexes of their databases — eg Data-Star.

The date of publication is also a factor which either widens or narrows the data produced and the costs entailed. Generally it is best to go backwards in time. There may be little point in obtaining a two-year-old report on plans to open a super quarry if, in the last month, a planning enquiry blocked the development.

Generally databases tell you the number of reports available before you commit yourself to the cost of down-loading. Some also let you list the report headlines or allow you to check the context of the keywords used in the search (this would have solved the problem of 'wet springs' in researching the mechanical spring market). Like the bears' porridge, the number of reports indicated may be judged to be either too much (with a lot of dross included) or too little (nothing of substance). In the former case you can change the search to home-in more specifically or if the initial output appears too little, you can widen up the search. Homing-in or widening-up depends on, as discussed, the number of databases accessed, keyword choice, degree of truncating and the time period covered. This is summarised, together with the consequences, in Figure 10.2.

PROBLEMS WITH ON-LINE DATABASES

The problem of database searching that can soon become transparent is the cost of going on-line. Every month, invoices will arrive from the hosts whose databases you have accessed. Without care, planning and skill in carrying out searches, these costs can get out of control. However, traditional desk research is not free if the researcher's time is realistically costed. A search may typically add up to £100 or £200 but do two days of a skilled researcher's time cost less? Also, used well, on-line database searching is very much more productive than library time. Typically two days spent in travelling, locating sources, note-taking and photocopying can be compressed into a couple of hours accessing on-line databases (and the majority of this time should be spent planning rather than logged onto the databases). On-line databases, therefore, make researchers very much more efficient. Also the costs of database searching can be controlled and reduced as the researcher gains experience and learns to plan searches carefully — it is definitely not just a button-pushing activity. Project budgeting should be used to control the costs of on-line database searches, even where this is purely an internal matter and does not involve a paying client.

Efficient use of on-line databases requires skills and, in turn, a commitment to training and having sufficient demand for information to acquire the necessary skills. Problems will certainly arise if unskilled staff are let loose on on-line database searches. These will not just be a matter of money, although the costs of poorly controlled access to databases will be painful enough. Database searching is also likely to be written off because the output is poor and often irrelevant to project needs. The solution is to ensure that access to databases is restricted to trained staff, and as already mentioned it is often better to have one specialist do the work or, where demand is very low, it may be better to contract-out database searching.

As discussed elsewhere, on-line databases do not yet cover all important market research sources. Particular omissions are parts of the trade press and some important statistical data. Total reliance on databases and the accompanying if-it-is-not-on-the-screen-it-doesn't-exist syndrome is, therefore, a potential problem. Market researchers should have a grounding in conventional desk sources and know when and where to look beyond on-line searches. However, what databases lack in coverage should not be over stated.

Linked to the above is the problem that on-line database searching can produce far too much data which, when it is reviewed, is found to be of little, if any, real value — research should produce actionable information, not undigested data; something considered in the next chapter. Where this problem arises, it often reflects poor search planning which, as stressed earlier, must be done before logging-on. In conventional research you can think about the data as you find it. This is not the case with on-line searching; once you have the data you have paid for it. In database research the thinking time needs to be up-front.

Finally, on-line databases cannot be 'browsed'. While for many purposes, database searching is a very effective method of locating and retrieving sources, it does not allow you to use that intuitive feel for information which, in conventional desk research, can sometimes produce a vital lead.

OTHER ELECTRONIC DATA

As an alternative to on-line access, some databases can be bought in disk or cd-rom form. Databases in disk form can be used on any office PC but cd-rom requires additional equipment that, as yet, is not commonly found in offices. Once purchased, the database can be accessed as often as required without incurring additional costs. There is also far less of a problem with unskilled access to the database; because there are no marginal costs, inefficient and unskilled searching leads to fewer cost penalties. As time goes by, the data will become outdated, but suppliers usually offer a regular up-dating service to overcome this problem (though not as completely as on-line databases).

Databases on disk or cd-rom media include some of the large directory databases and some statistical sources. Initial charges are substantial, but if use is frequent and on-going, savings are likely, compared to either on-line access or staff time involved in using conventional paper sources. This type of database is, therefore, appropriate where there is an identified need for regular and substantial use of the database. These conditions are probably less common in market research work than in such as credit checking and direct marketing. However, cd-rom (and linked multi-media technology) appears to be set for growth and their value, in market research, could change dramatically. Possibly, within a few years, many hard-copy directories and similar data sources may be widely available, and at lower prices, on cd-rom.

11

DESK RESEARCH REPORTING

The author once attended a meeting at which a market research executive presented the results of a large, important and strategic project. The table in the presentation room was loaded with papers. There were stacks of printouts, photocopies of articles, collections of product literature, several reports and some large directories. A rambling talk was then given, mentioning all the many sources used over the three-month study and with overhead slides of complex statistics shown. The industry behind the work could not be doubted but what it all added up to was not so clear. Probably the managers at the presentation are still wondering. This is not the way. The task of market researchers is to provide managers with clear information on which good decisions can be based. This is achieved by effective reporting and this is the subject of this final chapter.

Many of the basic principles of effective reporting are common to both desk research and fieldwork data and these are covered as well as some special aspects peculiar to desk research data.

TYPES OF REPORTS

Market research reports are often thought of as long, earnest but dull documents, dense with text and tables and of a thickness proportionate to the scale and cost of the research. Arguably this is all right because the reports are not written to give pleasure —

no one reads them unless they have to. However, too often, because of poor presentation, reports fail to make the impact they should. This is a pity and does not have to be the case.

Often the most effective form of reporting is a face-to-face presentation. At its simplest it is the researcher talking across a desk to a manager, but more formally it may involve an audience of some size. Few presenters at any sort of meeting can hold the attention of an audience and, therefore, effectively communicate, without visual aids of some sort. This is particulary so with market research data — even the simplest of statistics need to be shown. At a one-to-one meeting, visual aids can simply be tables and other material passed across the desk, but with larger audiences, overhead slides, a flip-chart or other material will be required. The audience will also want to take hard copy of key data away at the end — copies of overhead slides can usually well meet this need.

The presentation material, bound as a report, perhaps with an introduction and conclusions added, is effectively a written report and often provides sufficient record of the research project. Such a document may be a more effective and therefore better report than the traditional approach with full narrative — many decision-makers have neither the time nor the inclination to read a dense document. However, there is still a need for the full written report, particularly if the research results are to be communicated to readers who cannot attend a presentation meeting. Also, in commissioned research, both clients and research agencies often expect a full report to be provided; if nothing else, it has a symbolic value.

REPORT STRUCTURE

The main principles of report structure apply to presentation material as well as written reports and to the results of fieldwork as well as desk research.

At primary school you were perhaps taught that every story needs a beginning, a middle and an end. This is not a bad rule for market research reports. The beginning is an introduction, the middle is the findings of the research and the end is the conclusions. At least these elements ought to be present in all research reports, although there is a case for bringing the conclusions nearer to the front of a written report.

An *introduction* meets the reader's or audience's need to know why the research was carried out (background), what information was sought (objectives) and how it was obtained (research methods). With this out of the way, the findings can be understood in context.

The background element of the introduction needs to be only brief; a paragraph or even a sentence is usually sufficient eg:

> The Magnificent Marble Company is considering marketing a revolutionary style of slab and Truefacts were commissioned to carry out research on the potential acceptability of the new product.

The second part of the introduction should be the research objective and a listing of the main information areas covered to meet this objective. As argued in Chapter 2, every project should have formal, explicit objectives and a defined information coverage, written down in some form at the start of the research. At the reporting stage, therefore, there should be no difficulty stating what these were. If the research was wholly based on desk research, it is possible that some of the objectives were not fully covered because the data was simply unobtainable. If this is the case, this is the point in the report to say so and probably with a comment on the implications (eg the missing information is required before a final decision is taken and fieldwork research should be considered).

The final part of the introduction is a description of the methods used in the research. If fieldwork has been used this might be a substantial section (with details of sampling and interviewing techniques) but in a purely desk research study you can be quite brief eg:

> The information for this report was collected through desk research from published sources and by database searching. A list of the key sources is appended (Appendix 1).

Listing at least the important sources in this way is good practice, even though they should, as well, be given in the findings section.

In some reports it is considered useful to add a glossary of technical terms used in the report. There may be a case for this, but the contrary argument is that jargon, unfamiliar to the intended report audience, should not be used at all.

The research *findings* part of a report is very much the meat of the document; it is a presentation of the relevant data which has come out of the research. 'Relevant' is an important qualification. The data presented should meet the objectives of the research and not be thrown in just because you have come across it or even because it may be vaguely interesting. Findings are the facts meeting the objectives; no more and no less. Findings should also principally be statements of facts, rather than the report author's opinions. There is a place for the researcher to give an opinion, but it is not here. The facts may, of course, be others' opinions, where they are themselves significant in the market — eg opinions of buyers to the service provided by suppliers. However, the researcher should in such cases make sure that it is transparent whose opinions are being referred to (ie the market's and not the researcher's personal opinions). This can avoid some serious misunderstandings, particularly if negative views on a company's products or service standards are being reported.

Findings are statements of what is or what might be and not what ought to be. However, it is sometimes useful to provide some 'pointers' leading to the later conclusions. In the example below the 'pointer' is in bold text.

> The market has shrunk by an average of 2% per annum throughout the latter 1980s and early 1990s. **This fact may be relevant to the market entry decision**.

In findings of desk research, all the data will have come from one or more source and these should be explicitly referenced. The reader then knows the 'authority' of the data while a researcher can trace sources in any follow-on research. This is easy to do in the case of such as statistics. If the data in a table is from Business Monitor, the source can be shown at the bottom of the table (Business Monitor PAS 2600 1992) — do not forget to include the date and particularly, if it is not otherwise clear, to which period the data relates. Similarly, a press source might be quoted in the text:

It has been reported that OPEC is facing a collapse of oil prices. Current prices are already down to $16 a barrel. (*The Economist* 18 September 1993).

However, there are difficulties in attributing sources where a finding is an amalgam from several desk research sources. In this case it may be justifiable to be vague (eg press reports indicate . . .). Also where the findings are being presented as visual aids (and, therefore, of necessity concise and brief) it is justifiable to miss off source references but, if possible, they should appear on any material the audience take away.

The findings section of the report (whether written or verbal) should be organised in some logical sequence of subjects. In a market structure report, the order of the main headings might be:

1. Product analysis
2. Market size by sector
3. Past and recent trends
4. Suppliers and their market shares
5. Distribution
6. Marketing methods
7. Market forecasts

A report may include findings from both desk research and field-work. Bearing in mind that the audience for the report will generally be more interested in what has been found than how, it is better to integrate the findings by theme rather than have separate desk research and fieldwork sections. If, for example, desk research data includes market share estimates and fieldwork includes consumers' satisfaction with suppliers, the two subjects could come together in the 'suppliers' section of the report.

The purpose of the *conclusions* section of a report is often misunderstood, even by researchers claiming some experience. Conclusions are not a summary, although some of the main findings may be repeated. Nor are conclusions the same as recommendations; these go one step further and follow conclusions. Conclusions should tell the reader or audience the 'so what' of the research — significant implications of the findings. They are of course rooted in the facts, but go beyond and necessarily include opinion; the researcher's opinion. For example:

> The sector of the owner occupier market without central heating is predominantly found in the lower income groups (65% in the D and E social class group). This should be taken into account in developing new product packages and particularly in relation to pricing and finance deals.

In the example, the first sentence reiterates findings mentioned earlier in the report (with a proportion quoted in brackets to give authority to the statement). The second sentence, however, goes further and considers the implications and includes the report author's opinion.

To prepare effective conclusions the researcher needs an understanding of the interests and wider commercial objectives of the decision makers who are the report's audience (eg to increase sales of central heating appliances and particulary to first-time homes).

Beyond conclusions are recommendations eg:

> The Company should develop a simple central heating package to be installed at costs of under £700 and backed by low repayment finance deals.

In this case the report is not just stating the implications of the research, but is now saying specifically what should be done. If the recommendations are accepted, the company will be committed to action, expenditure and risk.

Making such recommendations requires an even greater understanding of the commercial environment, including areas well outside a market researcher's normal scope — eg whether the appliance can be sold profitably within the suggested price bands. Quite often the researcher lacks such additional knowledge and this is particularly the case in a research agency/client relationship. Moreover, the researcher may not need to make recommendations and possibly they might not even be welcome. After all, deciding policy is the responsibility of the managers for whom the report has been prepared. Therefore, before moving from conclusions to recommendations, the researcher should consider whether this is required — was it included or implied in the original research brief and objectives?

An introduction, findings and conclusions are the main elements in a market research report, whether it is verbal and face-to-face or a written document. Two other parts of a report are a summary and appendices. A *summary* is required in a written report of any length (eg if the findings are more than five pages). It should be short; no more than 5 per cent of the length of the findings. Often summaries are hastily written at the last minute. This is a mistake. The summary will often be more carefully read than the full report. Writing the summary is also a good test of the findings section — if you find it difficult to summarise large parts of the findings, it is probably because they do not say anything. It is not true that some findings are so complex (qualitative researchers say 'rich') that they cannot be summarised; they are almost certainly just waffle.

It is generally agreed that in written reports summaries are best bound at or near the front of the report, but precisely where is a matter of opinion. Some favour having the summary as the very first section in which case it should summarise the introduction and the conclusions as well as the findings. Others prefer a summary after the introduction and some recommend that the conclusions should follow (and precede the main findings). These are matters of personal preference.

Verbal presentations often do not include a summary. Where the range of data is quite small this is appropriate but if the research findings are complex and lengthy, there is a strong argument for summarising after discussing the findings in detail and before the conclusions are presented.

Appendices in written reports include material which the reader may wish to refer to but probably not initially. An appendix is a suitable place to list the sources consulted in desk research. Other possibilities include samples of product literature and possibly photocopies of particularly useful articles or tables of detailed statistics. In fieldwork research, the questionnaires are usually attached as an appendix. However, resist the temptation to include everything of the remotest interest found in the research. Such material can be kept on file rather than used to fill out the report to an unmanageable size.

PREPARING WRITTEN REPORTS

The building blocks of a written report are words/text, statistical tables and charts. As appropriate these are used to communicate the findings as well as the other elements of the report. The first step, however, should be to plan the report structure in some detail. Hasty or novice report writers are often in too much of a hurry to start writing. Quite likely they are up against a tight deadline and feel they are only making progress when words, tables and charts have been put on paper (or nowadays on the screen). The PC is also partly to blame; because it is so easy to correct, there is thought to be even less need for planning.

Lack of planning is nearly always evident and time spent in this way, at the front end, will lead to a better report. Moreover, with less revision and correction at the end, the report writing time will be no longer (it may even be less). The plan should consist of all the main headings within the report, with each then broken down into sub-headings and the information points listed under each. If the report is heavily statistical, it works well to prepare the tables or charts, arrange them in order to fit your plan and only then write the text (which will be mainly a commentary on the tables). With such an approach, the real thinking is done and you can give full attention to the writing task.

Reading a few paragraphs in this chapter cannot make you an expert author, but here are a few writing tips to consider:

- Keep your literary style plain and simple. Short sentences and simple familiar words. If you do not know your reader assume he or she takes the *Sun* and not *The Times*.
- Avoid jargon wherever possible unless you are certain that the report readers will be familiar with the terms.
- Keep paragraphs short — but not exclusively one-sentence paragraphs.
- The use of 'bullet points' such as these are often effective and break up otherwise long solid blocks of text.
- Write no more than you need — no waffle. If the research has found little (it sometimes happens), dressing it up in wordy paragraphs will not solve the problem.

■ Break up the main sections of the report with sub-headings eg:

— *Mainframe Market Shares*
or instead use headlines to focus attention eg:
— *IBM dominate the mainframe market*
Text is easier to read with sub-headings or headlines and there should be at least one heading per page.

■ In sections and paragraphs move from the general to the particular and from the most important statements to secondary information.

Numerical data should be presented in tables or charts. Both tables and charts should be fully understandable without reading any accompanying text. Tables, therefore, should have a title, both columns and rows labelled and units defined (%, £, numbers, tonnes etc). If values are shown as percentages, the 'base numbers' should be included: eg if the table shows percentage shares held of a market, the market value should be shown as the base number. The source of the data should be identified at the bottom of the table.

Any data presented as a table can also be shown as a chart, and many people find numerical information easier to understand in pictorial form. Charts are now easy to produce using one of the PC graphics packages available. Common forms of charts for numerical data include pie diagrams (eg for market shares), trend lines (eg market size over time), bar and split bar charts and histograms (eg for comparisons of magnitudes). Like tables, charts should be adequately titled and labelled and at least the major numerical values included (eg a pie diagram of market share should show in figures as well as pictorially the shares held of at least the major suppliers).

As well as numerical data, charts can be used to convey concepts — Figures 10.1 and 10.2 in the previous chapter are examples of this type of chart. Almost any concept can be presented in this way, but the chart should help understanding and not be mere decoration. Some PC graphics packages allow an enormous range of images and icons to be brought into a chart but whether the results always justify the effort is another matter.

Some concepts can be clarified through charts but others are better expressed in words.

In full narrative reports, the contents of tables and charts should be discussed in the text. However, the purpose of this is to draw attention to what is important in the chart or table and not to repeat all the information in words. For example, for a table or chart showing market shares, the accompanying text may highlight the market leader and perhaps comment on the position held by another company of particular interest (eg a potential acquisition). There is, however, no point in listing all the suppliers and giving the market share of each in the text, if this is readily apparent in the table or chart.

Text accompanying tables or charts is best placed first; the reader finds what is significant before going to the table or chart.

Arguably, a hand written report on scrap paper does all that is required. It is unlikely, however, to impress or enhance the reputation of the author. With computers, high quality printers and word processing software available in nearly all offices, there is really no excuse for a poor standard of written report presentation. Professional quality documents can now be put together with only the minimum of skill.

FACE-TO-FACE PRESENTATION

All face-to-face presentations of market research information benefit from visual aids. In a one-to-one meeting this might be no more than sheets passed across the desk, but where the audience is any larger, more elaborate aids are required. The choices include flip-charts (large pads of paper), overhead transparencies, 35mm slides and computer display. Flip-charts are very good to use in meetings to record ideas as they arise but less suitable for visual aids prepared in advance of the meeting, and have little to commend them if an overhead projector is available. Overhead transparencies are easy to produce on most plain paper copiers from paper originals (and these can also be copied on paper and given to the audience at the end of the presentation). 35mm slides provide very high quality visual aids but are expensive and not quick to produce. They are only justified for a really major presentation. Also, a presentation with 35mm slides has to be given in subdued lighting and does not encourage audience participation in the meeting. Computer-generated visual aids, projected onto a monitor or screen are likely to become increasingly important, but for the moment setting up the 'show' is more trouble and takes longer than with overhead transparencies.

Preparing really good visual aids needs as much thought and planning as for written reports. They can be in word, table or chart form but the most important requirement in each case is that they are understandable and legible to the audience. This means that they should be simple and that each slide should communicate only a limited amount of information. Text should be confined to a few lines of words or short phrases but should stand alone and be meaningful — not mere prompts to the presenter. Tables and charts should also be simple and include only detail which can be read easily by the audience. For this reason, the tables and charts (and even more so the text) of written reports may not be suitable to use, without modification, as visual aids.

While good visual aids add to a face-to-face presentation, they only support the presenter and will not make up for a poor performance. Again, it is vital to prepare thoroughly. Make notes of what you are going to say about each slide (mark up a paper copy). If you wish, write it all out verbatim but, if you do, never read it out word for word at the presentation. It always sounds flat and dull. Also, if you use text charts as visual aids talk about them and do not read them; if the audience cannot read them it is because they (either the charts or the audience) are unsuitable. It is better to hand out any paper copies of the visual aids at the end of the meeting since, if the audience have them at the start, they will be reading instead of listening to you.

When you first start making presentations you will be nervous — often the audience will be very much your seniors. Remember, though, that you know more about the research than they do. Speak slowly. Field questions as best you can but if you do not know the answers do not make it up; you will lose credibility. Lastly, try to enjoy your own performance.

12

LIST OF SOURCES

■

1. *Business Monitor*, HMSO Publications Centre, PO Box 276, London, SW8 5DT. Tel: 071-873 0011

2. *Which*, 2 Marylebone Road, London, NW1 4DF. Tel: 071-486 5544

3. *Annual Abstract of Statistics*, HMSO (see ref 1)

4. *Social Trends*, HMSO (see ref 1)

5. *National Readership Survey*, Joint Industry Committee For National Readership Surveys, 44 Belgrave Square, London, SW1X 8Q2. Tel: 071-235 7020

6. *Marketing Pocket Book*, NTC Publications, Farm Road, Henley-on-Thames, Oxfordshire, RG9 1EJ. Tel: 0491 574671

7. *CACI Ltd*, Kensington Village, Avonmore Road, London, W14 8TS. Tel: 071-602 6000

8. *Kompass*, Reed Information Services, Windsor Court, East Grinstead, West Sussex, RH19 1XA. Tel: 0342 326972

9. *Guide to Official Statistics*, HMSO (see ref 1)

10. *British Library*, Southampton Building, Chancery Lane, London, WC2A 2AW. Tel: 071-323 7454 also: Document Supply Centre, Boston Spa, Wetherby, West Yorkshire, LS23 7BQ. Tel: 0937 546229

11. *Financial Times Business Research Centre*, 1 Southwark Bridge, London, SE1 9HL. Tel: 071-873 4102

12. *ASLIB*, 20 Old Street, London, EC1V 9AP. Tel: 071-253 4488

13. *CSO Newport Library And Information Service*, Cardiff Road, Newport, Gwent, NP9 1XG. Tel: 0633 812973

14. *Dti Export Marketing Information Centre*, Ashdown House, 123 Victoria Street, London, SW1E 5ED. Tel: 071-215 5444

15. *SMMT*, Forbes House, Halkin Street, London, SW1X 7DS. Tel: 071-235 7000

16. *Directory of British Associations*, CBD Research, 15 Wickham Road, Beckenham, Kent, BR3 2JS. Tel: 081-650 7745

17. *Business Statistics (Clinch)*, Headland Press, 1 Henry Smith's Terrace, Headland, Cleveland, TS24 0PD. Tel: 0429 231902

18. *Market Search*, Arlington Publications, 25 New Bond Street, London, W1Y 9HD. Tel: 071-495 1940

19. *Marketing Surveys Index*, Marketing Strategies For Industry, 19 Heathmans Road, Parsons Green, London, SW6 4TJ. Tel: 071-371 0955

20. *Reports Index*, Business Surveys Ltd, Osmington Drive, Broadmayne, Dorset, DT2 8ED. Tel: 0305 853704

21. *Findex*, available through Euromonitor (see ref 25)

22. *Frost & Sullivan*, 4 Grosvenor Gardens, London, SW1W 0DH. Tel: 071-730 3438

23. *Mintel*, Mintel International Group, 18 Long Lane, London, EC1A 9HE. Tel: 071-606 4533

24. *Retail Business*, Economists Intelligence Unit, 40 Duke Street, London, W1A 1DU. Tel: 071-493 6711

25. *Euromonitor*, 87 Turnmill Street, London, EC1 5QU. Tel: 071-251 8025

26. *TGI,* BMRB International, Hadley House, 79 Uxbridge Road, Ealing, London, W5 5SU. Tel: 081-566 5000

27. *AGB,* The Research Centre, West Gate, London, W5 1UA. Tel: 081-967 0007

28. *Nielsen,* London Road, Headington, Oxford, OX3 9RX. Tel: 0865 742742

29. *Research Index,* Business Surveys Ltd. (see ref 20)

30. *Monthly Index to the Financial Times,* Research Publications International, PO Box 45, Reading, RG1 8HF. Tel: 0734 583247

31. *BRAD,* Maclean Hunter Limited, Chalk Lane, Cockfosters Road, Barnet, Herts, EN4 0BU. Tel: 081-975 9759

32. *Pims,* Pims UK Ltd, 4 St John's Place, London, EC1M 4AH. Tel: 071-250 0870

33. *PR Planner,* 290 Green Lanes, London, N13 5TP. Tel: 081-882 0155

34. *Key British Enterprises,* Dun & Bradstreet, Holmers Farm Way, High Wycombe, Bucks, HP12 4UL. Tel: 0494 422000

35. *Kellys,* Reed Information Services. (see ref 8)

36. *Yellow Pages,* BT Phonebook Group, 25 Church Street, Manchester, M60 1BJ. Tel: 061-969 3666

37. *Current British Directories,* CBD Research. (see ref 16)

38. *Extel,* Extel Financial Information Centre, 13 Epworth Street, London, EC2A 4DL. Tel: 071-251 3333

39. *UK Marketing Source Book,* NTC Publications. (see ref 6)

40. *The Source Book,* Keynote Publications, 72 Oldfield Road, Hampton, Middlesex, TW12 2HQ. Tel: 081-783 0955

41. *Market Research — Guide To British Library Holdings,* British Library. (see ref 10)

42. *United Kingdom National Accounts,* HMSO. (see ref 1)

43. *United Kingdom Balance of Payments*, HMSO. (see ref 1)

44. *Economic Trends*, HMSO. (see ref 1)

45. *Monthly Digest of Statistics*, HMSO. (see ref 1)

46. *Regional Trends*, HMSO. (see ref 1)

47. *Central Statistics Office*, Great George Street, London, SW1P 4AQ. Tel: 071-270 6386

48. *Financial Times*, 1 Southwark Bridge, London, SE1 9AL. Tel: 071-873 3000

49. *The Economist*, 25 St James's Street, London, SW1A 1HG. Tel: 071-839 7000

50. *Henley Centre for Forecasting*, 2 Tudor Street, Blackfriars, London, EC4Y 0AA. Tel: 071-353 9961

51. *London Business School*, Sussex Place, Regent's Park, London, NW1 4SA. Tel: 071-724 2300

52. *OECD*, 2 Rue Andre-Pascal, 75775 Paris, France. (publications also from HMSO — see ref 1)

53. *Retail Prices*, HMSO. (see ref 1)

54. *Census of Population*, HMSO (see ref 1) and OPCS, Segensworth Road, Tichfield, Fareham, Hampshire, PO15 5RR. Tel: 0329 813800

55. *Introductory Guide to the 1991 Census*, NTC Publications. (see ref 6)

56. *Harvest*, Mintel International Group. (see ref 23)

57. *Family Expenditure Survey*, HMSO. (see ref 1)

58. *General Household Survey*, HMSO. (see ref 1)

59. *Lifestyle Pocket Book*, NTC Publications. (see ref 6)

60. *Lifestyle trends in the UK*, J Walter Thompson, 40 Berkeley Square, London, W1X 6AD. Tel: 071-497 4040

61. *Targeting Adults*, Marketing Strategies For Industry. (see ref 19)

62. *Consumer Market Factfile*, Euromonitor. (see ref 25)

63. *Standard Industrial Classification of Economic Activities*, HMSO. (see ref 1)

64. *Investors Chronicle*, Greystoke Place, Fetter Lane, London, EC4A 1ND. Tel: 071-405 6969

65. *McCarthy Information*, Manor House, Ash Walk, Warminster, Wilts, BA12 8LX. Tel: 0985 215151

66. *Market Research GB*, Euromonitor. (see ref 25)

67. *Keynote* (see ref 40)

68. *ICC Business Ratio Reports*, ICC, 72 Oldfield Road, Hampton, Middlesex, TW12 2HQ. Tel: 081-783 0922

69. *Market Assessment of Top Markets*, Market Assessment Publications, 2 Duncan Terrace, London, N1 8BZ. Tel: 071-278 9517

70. *Market Forecasts*, Market Assessment Publications. (see ref 69)

71. *Market Size Digest*, Mintel. (see ref 23)

72. *Tradstat*, Plaza Suite, 114 Jermyn Street, London, SW1Y 6HJ. Tel: 071-930 5503

73. *Marketing*, 30 Lancaster Gate, London, W2 3LP. Tel: 071-413 4150

74. *Marketing Week*, St Giles House, 50 Poland Street, London, WN 4AX. Tel: 071-439 4222

75. *Advertising Statistics Yearbook*, Advertising Association, 15 Wilton Road, London, SW1V 1NJ. Tel: 071-828 2771

76. *MEAL*, St Martin's Lane, London, WC2N 4JT. Tel: 071-240 1903

77. *Who Owns Whom*, Dun & Bradstreet. (see ref 34)

78. *Market Location*, 1 Warwick Street, Leamington Spa, Warwickshire, CV32 5LW. Tel: 0926 450388

79. *Circare*, 108 Leonard Street, London, EC2A 4RH. Tel: 071-739 8424

80. *ICC Group*. (see ref 68)

81. *Dun & Bradstreet*. (see ref 34)

82. *Infocheck*, Infocheck Group, Godmersham Park, Godmersham, Canterbury, Kent, CT4 7DT. Tel: 0227 813000

83. *CIPFA*, 3 Robert Street, London, WC2N 6BH. Tel: 081-667 1144

84. *Glass's Car Guide*, Elgin House, St George's Avenue, Weybridge, Surrey, KT13 0BX. Tel: 0932 853211

85. *What to Buy For Business*, 27 Park Street, Croydon, Surrey, CR0 1YD. Tel: 081-680 2828

86. *BSI*, British Standards Institution, Linford Wood, Milton Keynes, MK14 6LE. Tel: 0908 226888

87. *Dti Hotline*. Phone enquiries: 0272 444888

88. *Spearhead*, Dti European database accessible through various hosts including FT Profile (see ref 136)

89. *ABCC*, 4 Westwood House, Westwood Business Park, Coventry, CV4 8HS. Tel: 0203 694484

90. *European Information Centres*, Centres are throughout the UK eg: Department Of Employment, Ebury Gate, London, SW1 8QD. Tel: 071-730 8451

91. *The Guide*, Keynote. (see ref 40)

92. *European Directory of Marketing Information Sources*, Euromonitor. (see ref 25)

93. *European Directory of Non Official Statistics*, Euromonitor. (see ref 25)

94. *Published Data on European Industry Markets*, Industrial Aids, 14 Buckingham Palace Road, London, SW1P 0QP. Tel: 071-828 5036

95. *Guide to European Market Information*, London Business School. (see ref 51)

96. *Directory of International Sources of Business Information* (Ball). Pitman Publishers, 128 Long Acre, London, WC2E 9AN. Tel: 071-379 7383

97. *Statistical Sources* (Wasserman & Wasserman), Gale Research International, PO Box 699, North Way, Andover, Hants, SP10 5YE. Tel: 0246 334446

98. *Benn's Media Directory International*, Benn Business Information Service, PO Box 20, Tonbridge, Kent, TN9 1SE. Tel: 0732 362666

99. *European Directory of Trade and Business Journals*, Euromonitor. (see ref 25)

100. *Directory of European Industrial and Trade Associations*, CBD Research. (see ref 16)

101. *European Directory of Consumer Market Reports and Surveys*, Euromonitor. (see ref 25)

102. *European Product and Market Reports*, DATA Group, 207 Desborough Road, High Wycombe, Bucks, HP11 2QL. Tel: 0494 450305

103. *Marketing in Europe*, Economists Intelligence Unit. (see ref 24)

104. *European Retail*, Economists Intelligence Unit. (see ref 24)

105. *Market Research Europe*, Euromonitor. (see ref 25)

106. *European Marketing Pocket Book*, NTC Publications. (see ref 6)

107. *European Marketing Data and Statistics*, Euromonitor. (see ref 25)

108. *European Compendium of Marketing Information*, Euromonitor. (see ref 25)

109. *Consumer Europe*, Euromonitor. (see ref 25)

110. *European Market Share Reporter*, Gale Research International. (see ref 97)

111. *Predicast*, 8-10 Denham Street, London, W1V 7RF. Tel: 071-494 3817

112. *European Advertising Marketing and Media*, Euromonitor. (see ref 25)

113. *European Advertising and Media Forecast*, NTC Publications. (see ref 6)

114. *World Advertising Expenditure*, NTC Publications. (see ref 6)

115. *Economists Intelligence Unit*. (see ref 24)

116. *Index of Articles Published*, Predicast. (see ref 111)

117. *Eurostat*, Directorate A, L-2920, Luxembourg. Tel: 4301 4567

118. *Eurostat Index* (Ramsay) Capital Planning Information, St Martins, Stamford, Lincs, PE 9 2LG. Tel: 0780 57300

119. *United Nations Information Centre*, Ship House, 20 Buckingham Gate, London, SW1 6LD. Tel: 071-630 1981

120. *Bureau of The Census*, Customer Services, Washington, DC 20233, USA. Tel: 301 763 4100

121. *Statistical Abstract of the US*, Bureau of The Census. (see ref 120)

122. *Census of Manufacturing*, Bureau of The Census. (see ref 120)

123. *US Industrial Outlook*, US Department Of Commerce, Washington, DC 20230, USA. Tel: 202 377 4901

124. *Guide to Federal Data Sources on Manufacturing*, US Department Of Commerce. (see ref 123)

125. *American Statistics Index*, Congressional Information Service, Bathesda, Maryland 20814, USA.

126. *Thomas Register of American Manufacturers*, 1 Penn Plaza, New York 10001, USA. Tel: 212 695 0500

127. *Major Companies of Europe*, Graham & Trotman, Sterling House, 66 Wilton Road, London, SW1V 1DE. Tel: 071-821 1123

128. *Sourceguide to European Company Information* (Scott/London Business School), Gale International Research. (see ref 97)

129. *Jordans*, St Thomas Street, Bristol, BS1 6JS. Tel: 0272 230600

130. *On Line Business Sourcebook*, Headland Press. (see ref 17)

131. *On Line Business and Company Databases* (Parkinson), ASLIB. (see ref 12)

132. *On Line Management and Marketing Databases* (Parker), ASLIB. (see ref 12)

133. *Directory of On Line Databases*, Gale Research International. (see ref 97)

134. *WEFA*, Ebury Gate, 23 Lower Belgrave, London, SW1W 0NW. Tel: 071-730 8171

135. *Data-Star*, Plaza Suite, 114 Jermyn Street, London, SW1Y 6HJ. Tel: 071-930 5503

136. *FT Profile*, PO Box 12, Sunbury on Thames, Middlesex, TW16 7UD. Tel: 0932 761444

137. *Dialog Information Services*, PO Box 188, Oxford, OX1 5AX. Tel: 0865 730725

138. *BMRB*. (see ref 26)

139. *MAID Systems*, 26 Baker Street, London, W1M 1DF. Tel: 071-935 6460

BIBLIOGRAPHY

∎

GENERAL READING ON MARKET RESEARCH (CONSUMER RESEARCH ORIENTATED)

Aaker, David A & George S Day (1990) *Marketing Research*, John Wiley, Chichester.

Baker, Michael J (1991) *Research for Marketing*, Macmillan, London.

Birn, R, Hague, P and Vangelder, P, (eds) (1990) *A Handbook of Market Research Techniques*, Kogan Page, London.

Birn, Robin (1991) *The Effective Use of Market Research*, Kogan Page, London.

Cannon, Tom (1973) *Advertising Research*, Intertext, Aylesbury.

Chisnall, Peter (1991) *The Essence of Marketing Research*, Prentice-Hall, Englewood Cliffs, New Jersey.

Chisnall, Peter (1992) *Marketing Research*, McGraw-Hill, Maidenhead.

Crimp, Margaret (1990) *The Marketing Research Process*, Prentice-Hall, Englewood Cliffs, New Jersey.

Crouch, S (1984) *Marketing Research for Managers*, Heinemann, Oxford.

Ehrenberg, ASC (1988) *Repeat Buying*, Edward Arnold, Sevenoaks.

Gordon, Wendy & Roy Langmaid (1988) *Qualitative Market Research*, Gower, Aldershot.

Gorton, Keith & Isobel Doole (1989) *Low-Cost Marketing Research*, John Wiley & Sons, Chichester.

Green, P & Tull, J (1978) *Research for Marketing Decisions*, Prentice-Hall, Englewood Cliffs, New Jersey.

Hague, Paul N & Peter Jackson (1990) *How To Do Marketing Research*, Kogan Page, London.

Hague, Paul N & Peter Jackson (1987) *Do Your Own Market Research*, Kogan Page, London.

Jain, AK, Pinson, P & Ratchford, B (1982) *Marketing Research — Applications and Problems*, John Wiley & Sons, Chichester.

Kreuger, Richard A (1989) *Focus Groups (A Practical Guide For Small Businesses)*, Sage Publications, London.

Robson, S & Foster, A (eds) (1989) *Qualitative Research in Action*, Edward Arnold, Sevenoaks.

Talmage, PA (1988) *Dictionary of Marketing Research*, Market Research Society, London.

Walker, R (ed) (1985) *Applied Qualitative Research*, Gower, Aldershot.

Williams, Keith (1981) *Behavioural Aspects of Marketing*, Heinemann, Oxford.

Worcester, RM & Downam, J (eds) (1986) *Consumer Market Research Handbook*, Elsevier, Netherlands.

GENERAL READING ON INDUSTRIAL MARKET RESEARCH

Hague, Paul N & Peter Jackson (1992) *Marketing Research in Practice*, Kogan Page, London.

MacLean, Ian (ed) (1976) *Handbook of Industrial Marketing Research*, Kluwer-Harrap, Brentford.

Stacey, NAH & Aubrey Wilson (1963) *Industrial Market Research — Management Techniques*, Hutchinson, London.

Sutherland, Ken (ed) (1991) *Researching Business Markets*, Kogan Page in association with the Industrial Marketing Research Association, London.

Wilson, Aubrey (1968) *The Assessment of Industrial Markets*, Hutchinson, London.

QUESTIONNAIRES

Hague, Paul (1993) *Questionnaire Design*, Kogan Page, London.

Openheim, AN (1970) *Questionnaire Design and Attitude Measurement*, Heinemann, Oxford.

Wolfe, A (1984) *Standardised Questions*, Market Research Society, London.

PRESENTATIONS AND REPORT WRITING

Jay, Anthony (1976) *Slide Rules*, Video Arts, London.

May, John (1982) *How To Make Effective Business Presentations*, McGraw-Hall, London.

JOURNALS AND PERIODICALS

Business Marketing Digest, (formerly *Industrial Marketing Digest*), quarterly, Wallington, Surrey.

Harvard Business Review, bi-monthly, Boston, Mass, US.

Journal of The Market Research Society, quarterly, London.

Marketing, weekly, London.

INDEX

■